PSYCHOLINGUISTICS

James Deese
The Johns Hopkins University

Allyn and Bacon, Inc.
Boston · London · Sydney

ISBN: 0-205-02445-9

Seventh printing . . . March, 1975

PREFACE

During the past few years, psycholinguistics has become an important and intellectually significant part of modern psychology. Psycholinguistics can be described as the search for ways of characterizing certain intellectual abilities of human beings in order to account for the extraordinary facts of language and the use of language by human beings. The chief ideas in psycholinguistics come from modern linguistic theory, and they are not yet familiar to many students of psychology or even some teachers of psychology. This book is meant to introduce psycholinguistic ideas to psychologists unacquainted with them.

The book makes no assumptions about the backgrounds of its readers, and can be read by a person unfamiliar with linguistics or psycholinguistics, though it is meant to be read from the cultural viewpoint of psychology. Except for the fact that the book provides only a short introduction to the field of psycholinguistics, no attempt has been made to gloss over difficulties of the subject matter. The result may be that some readers find that parts of the book require careful study rather than casual reading. Those sections difficult for the reader deserve special study, and perseverance in them should be rewarded by understanding of a new and different approach to the psychology of language. There is nothing in them which requires particularly specialized knowledge. Readers already familiar with modern linguistic theory will find those sections to be summaries of what they know already.

The first chapter contains an outline of modern linguistic theory as it applies to psycholinguistics. This chapter is absolutely essential for those readers who are unfamiliar with psycholinguistics. The reader should be certain that he is familiar with the concepts in it before he attempts the succeeding chapters. Once it has been studied, however, the remaining chapters can be read with profit in almost any order. The student who is taking introductory psychology may prefer to read the last chapter first, while the student of experimental psychology will almost certainly be interested in the second chapter.

The second chapter is an account of some recent experiments on use and understanding of language. These experiments mainly have been inspired by modern linguistic theory, and they are meant to examine linguistic theory as a kind of theory of human linguistic performance. The third chapter is an account of some features of the development of language in children. This chapter relies very heavily on the material presented in Chapter One, and the student who attempts to study it should make certain that he is familiar with the material in Chapter One. This chapter makes no attempt to provide a complete chronological account of linguistic development, but only to show how psycholinguistic theory and research may illuminate our understanding of processes at work in that chronology.

The fourth chapter comes closest to being something that can be understood in its own right without dependence upon the material in Chapter One. However, the information in that chapter needs to be appreciated in the context of the linguistic theory presented in the first chapter. Also, the fourth chapter is the one in the book that comes closest to presenting some unique views. Much of the material in this chapter is based upon work performed by the author under NIH grant MH 06550. At the same time, it summarizes empirical methods and other theories of meaning. The final chapter places the psychology of language in its social and biological contexts. It draws heavily upon the views of E. H. Lenneberg and upon the recent work of sociolinguists.

Since this book provides only a brief introduction, the student may be interested in reading in greater depth in various aspects of psycholinguistics. Therefore, a short annotated list of books is presented at the end of the book in addition to the usual reference list.

James Deese

TABLE OF CONTENTS

LIST OF ILLUSTRATIONS

1.

THE NATURE
OF LANGUAGE

A language is a set of sentences. The English language consists of all those sentences that *could be* spoken in English. Intuition tells us that the set of sentences for any natural language, such as English, is very large, in fact infinite. People can think and say an indefinite number of different English sentences. No matter how many sentences have actually been said in any natural language, it is always possible to think of a new one. Each of the infinite number of sentences in a natural language is based upon a system of rules. The system of rules is the grammar of the language. The function of the grammar of a language is to enable us to map meanings onto sequences of sounds—to put what we think into words. Grammar is the essential link in communication between meaning and sound or meaning and symbol. Grammar provides the means whereby one person's thoughts may become another's. Meaning itself exists apart from and prior to particular sentences. The sounds and the written symbols that express meaning, on the other hand, are always parts of sentences. Once meaning has been mapped onto a sentence, that

1

sentence has some semantic interpretation. It says something. Thus, another way of looking at grammar is to say that it is the system of rules whereby more or less arbitrary strings of sounds or symbols can occur in such a way as to mean something. When meaning is made manifest in language it may be said to be semantic. Thus the concepts meaning and semantics are not synonymous.

The Importance of Grammar

There are other ways of looking at language. In fact, much of the above comes from a new theory of language. That theory is due mainly to the work of the American linguist, Noam Chomsky, and is called variously, generative theory, transformational theory, or even simply grammatical theory. Generative theory, as we shall call it, contains some old truths about language and shows us some important new ones. The most significant function it has had in the past decade, however, has been to provide our ideas about language with a firm theoretical foundation. It is the best and most powerful device available for telling us what we are talking about when we talk about language. Generative theory gives us the means of characterizing those things that are really essential to language in a precise and detailed way. It is not too much to say that no adequate account of the nature of language was possible before generative theory.

Not all psychologists know about generative theory, and of those who do, some are hostile to it. Some people regard it as being contradictory to learning theory, and learning theory has a central place in modern psychology. However, generative theory is only contrary to learning theory when learning theory is misapplied, as it sometimes is, to language. One of the consequences of the development of generative theory has been to show that learning theory, when it is carefully and strictly interpreted, as any good theory should be, cannot apply to the way in which people acquire, use, and understand ordinary human languages. Those who have tried to apply learning theory to the problem of how people use languages do not really understand what language really is. That is one reason why it is necessary to begin this book with a thorough account of *the nature of language*. Once we understand what language is, we can easily see that any version of learning theory—no matter how sophisticated—lacks the power to describe the most essential parts of language.

It is a mistake to suppose, however, that it is only learning theorists and other psychologists who have a faulty conception of language. Many linguists still cherish inadequate ideas about it. One of the misconceptions favored by almost an entire generation of American linguists is that one can study language without basic premises. According to such a view, the proper way to discover the system of rules (the grammar) of an unknown language would be (1) to discover the basic sound elements of the language (its phonemes) and then (2) discover the rules by which these elements are combined to form sentences. Generative theory shows that this scheme for analyzing languages is in error. No one can discover the basic "elements" of a language without knowing the rules for combining those elements. The elements, in fact, are the result of the rules, not the other way around. The most basic idea in the whole of the study of language is that of the sentence. We must start the investigation of language by characterizing the nature of the sentence rather than trying to find how individual sounds or words combine to compose sentences. An analogy (only partly correct as with all analogies) will help explain why. It is as if someone argued that it would be possible to construct a particular house simply by combining bricks, wood, mortar, nails, and pipes more or less by trial and error until the result looked like what one imagined the house should be. Generative theorists show that in order to describe a particular house (a language) we must have the plans first, and that these plans must conform to universal characteristics of all plans.

The Distinction between Language and Speech

Language occasionally is identified with the act of speaking, with the sounds made in speaking, or with both. That is a mistake.

Language is the most important aspect of, and in a sense the cause of speech, but it is not identical to speech. The English language is not simply the sum total of all the speech sounds made by speakers of English, though most of those speech sounds are determined by the language in one way or another. Perhaps the most famous distinction between language and speech is that made by the French linguist, Ferdinand de Saussure (1857–1913). Saussure distinguished between *la langue*, which is the system—both grammatic and semantic— that makes speech possible, and *la parole*, which is the actual vocal output of a speaker. He drew a parallel between the actual, spoken sentences in a language and the performance of a symphony. A symphony is both an abstract musical structure and an actual performance. Particular performances differ from one another and in important ways from the structure conceived by the composer. Musicians make mistakes, and conductors impose idiosyncratic interpretations. Thus it is with speech and language. There is an abstract structure which conforms to the system of the language, but a particular speaker deviates from that structure in actually speaking. A common cause of such deviation is limitation of memory. We sometimes start a sentence with a particular structure but half way through forget the basic scheme for that structure. The result is that we finish that sentence with a different structure. The complete sentence, then, is a hybrid between two linguistic structures. The influence of human limitations and similar problems make it absolutely essential that we maintain the distinction between language and speech and that we do not, as some psychologists have thought we should, identify language with the behavior of speaking or with the sounds produced by such behavior.

What Language Is Not

It is necessary to be absolutely clear about what language is not, for if we have a faulty conception of language, we cannot understand modern psycholinguistics. Linguistic performance is not, for example, the running off or performance of a set of conditioned responses or associations. If we were to argue that a sentence is nothing more than a complicated kind of conditioned response (as has been suggested; see Mowrer, 1954, for example) or a set of associations, or some more complicated version of these via the principle of mediation (see Osgood, 1968), we would be asserting (1) that each element in a sentence is a reaction to some preceding stimulus, and (2) these reactions are chained together in a string. There are several ways of showing that these two propositions are false (Chomsky, 1956). We shall allude to some of the proofs later. For now we need only recognize the impoverishment of the view of language which derives from these conceptions.

These notions imply that every sentence we speak is composed either of a sequence of unlearned or learned reactions. We are equipped at birth with a finite number of unlearned reactions (roughly, by unlearned reactions we mean something like a knee jerk) and surely, in a limited lifetime, we can only learn a finite number of new associations or conditioned responses. These learned reactions can be extended by stimulus and response generalization, but they still are finite in number, for there is a limited number of stimuli to which generalization occurs (you may remember that it decreases in strength as stimuli are less similar to the original conditioned stimulus) and a limited number of generalized responses. Therefore, unless we are at the moment learning a new association, we are limited to saying and interpreting what we have already said or heard. Yet the most important aspect of language is that it is creative. We can and do in almost every sentence that is not a stereotyped cliché say what has never been said before. Nor is what we say when we say something new simply a random or stochastic perturbation of our fixed associations. When we say something new we say it according to the system of rules that is the language. In short, the essential features of sentences are determined by rules, not by conditioned reactions. That is not to say that conditioning and similar processes do not influence aspects of speech, but it is to say that the essential part of speech—that which sets the act of speaking apart from other behavior—is based upon the rule-bearing character of language.

Competence and Performance

Chomsky (1965) makes a distinction between competence and performance that is in many ways similar to the distinction between *la langue* and *la parole*. Chomsky's distinction is a psychological one, however. He points out that each of us possesses some competence for language. Each of our heads evidently contains a device that can both generate and interpret sentences according to rules. There is, then, some embodiment of the abstract rules of language, and this embodiment is psychological and, we must suppose, neurophysiological. Performance on the other hand is simply an account of what we actually do. Our speech is determined by habit and a host of other things unrelated to linguistic competence. We greet one another by some standard phrase, such as, *"How do you do."* Parrots can and often do greet people in much the same way and perhaps for the same reasons. Parrots, however, have no competence for language. They cannot produce an indefinite number of sentences in the language. Such stereotyped sentences as those in greetings may or may not be a part of the language. As spoken by a parrot they are definitely not. We shall see later that many important psychological aspects of speaking are not part of linguistic competence, but this does not change the central fact that a psychological theory of language must describe something that corresponds to the rule structure of language.

SOUNDS AND LANGUAGE

By saying that conditioning and similar processes do not apply to language, we rule out any notion that asserts that sentences, sounds, words, or units at any level of language are learned as individual items, responses or sequences of responses. The older psychological textbooks on human development were quite positive on the topic of language development, and as wrong as they were positive. They asserted that children first learned to discriminate speech sounds from other sounds (babies were said to "learn to recognize human voices"), and then they learned to tell the different speech sounds apart. Next they learned to understand and say a few words, and then finally they were able to put these words together in basic "sentence-patterns." The rest of language development was said to be simply a matter of increasing the size of the vocabulary and learning ever more complicated schemes for fitting words into sentences. The fundamental error of this account can be illustrated by describing something of what we now know about how people tell speech sounds apart.

In theory, all babies have to learn to distinguish among speech sounds by the physical characteristics of those sounds. We all know that instances of particular speech sounds differ from one another. Some people—in the United States mainly among those from the Eastern seaboard—tend to reduce or drop the /r/[1] following vowels (as in "fathah" for father). Other people make the postvocalic /r/ loud and clear. Yet, we suppose, there must be some physical aspect of the sound of /r/ that remains the same from dialect to dialect and from instance to instance, or else we would not be able to identify it as such. Put another way, there must be some aspect of the acoustic signal that remains physically invariant through all of the variations of /r/.

The Nature of Sound Patterns

The past twenty years have produced a mountain of research on speech sounds, and some of that research has gone to weaken our faith in the idea that there must be some physically invariant aspect of speech sounds responsible for our ability to identify them. Much of this research has come from the use of the sound spectrograph and devices associated with it. A sound spectrograph represents sounds in two dimensions. One of these dimensions is the frequency of com-

---

[1] The conventional way to indicate the phonemes of speech is by setting them between diagonal lines. This convention is followed here, though following the lead provided by Chomsky and Halle (1968), we shall make restricted use of the concept of the phoneme.

ponents of the sound and the other is time. The sound spectrograph
shows how the frequencies of speech change with respect to time. A
sample sound-spectrograph is reproduced in Figure 1. Intensity of
any given frequency at any given time is represented by the degree
of darkening of that portion of the graph. Another instrument, the
pattern-playback device, "reads" sound-spectrograph records and
converts them to sound. With this device it is possible to produce

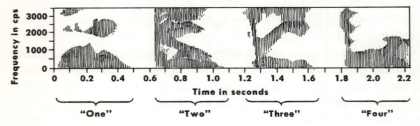

FIGURE 1.
A Sketch of a Spectrographic Record for the Words "One," "Two,"
"Three," and "Four." (From J. R. Steinberg and N. R. French, Journal
of the Acoustical Society of America, vol. 18, 4-18. Reprinted by permission of the publisher.)

sounds that have never actually been recorded. Instead of recording
a sound, someone can draw in india ink a pattern like that in Figure
1. Such patterns produce artificial speech.

In theory, the child learns to distinguish between sound patterns
like those pictured in Figure 1. For example, he is supposed to learn
to distinguish the /p/ of pit and the /b/ of bit mainly by the fact
that there is not a darkening of the record near the bottom for /p/,
while there is for /b/. The darkening at the bottom for /b/ is the
result of low frequency sounds emitted when the vocal cords vibrate.
The vocal cords vibrate for /b/ but not for /p/. One sound is said
to be voiced while the other is unvoiced. However, not all speakers
are careful about how they turn their vocal cords off and on. Some
speakers may make much the same sound for /p/ as for /b/. Many
speakers of Pennsylvania Dutch dialect do this.

The result of such confusion is that precisely the same acoustic
signal can be interpreted as two different phonemes on different

occasions. Or alternatively, the same physical signal may have to do double duty. In the most general case there is no invariant physical aspect common to all the different instances of each and every phoneme in English. The perception of speech is not simply a matter of detecting a physical signal. A more dramatic way to put this is to say that *there is no physical stimulus* for any given speech sound. A purely mechanical device could not, as a person can, translate speech sounds into a typescript. A typewriter that operates by voiced instructions is impossible.[2] It is impossible because there is no acoustic stimulus uniquely associated with a given speech sound. What we hear as speech sounds is a result partly of external stimulation and a result partly of knowledge already in our heads. An essential component of that knowledge is the grammar of the language we speak. A voice typewriter would have to have stored in the memory of its associated computer the general principles of English grammar before it could operate as effectively as an ordinary typist in typing dictation. It is not possible, at present, to program a computer for a thoroughly adequate English grammar. In general, we can sum up the dependence of the perception of speech on knowledge by saying that it depends on context.

The Perception of Speech

The influence of context can be illustrated by some simple experimental observations. In one experiment (Cooper, Borst, and Liberman, 1952) an artificial sound, which consisted of a short burst in the region of 1440 cycles per second, preceded a vowel sound like the vowel of *pit*, and in another case the same sound preceded the vowel sound like that of *putt*. In the first case, listeners identified one

---

[2] Some readers may object that such a device actually exists. It does, but it can transcribe the speech of only a trained speaker and only when that speaker pronounces a restricted vocabulary in an exceedingly careful way. No device now in existence can type accurately from my dictation (no matter how slow), but any ordinary speaker of English who types can. Nor is it simply a matter of English orthography. The same situation holds for Spanish or Czech or any other language with good correspondence between letters (graphemes) and sounds (phonemes).

burst as /p/ and in the second case they identified it as /k/. In this case, the words so identified would have been *pit* and *cut*. Thus, the same physical signal was identified as two different speech sounds depending upon the following vowel. In another example (Liberman, Harris, Kinney and Lane, 1961) it was possible to change identification of an artificial signal from /do/ to /to/ by a tiny change in the vowel—not the initial consonant. The change consisted in varying the onset time of one of the formants of the vowel. A formant is one of the two stable frequencies associated with each vowel in the speech of a given speaker. In phonological theory, the difference between /d/ and /t/ is supposed to be only a matter of voicing, just like the difference between /b/ and /p/. Yet in this case, whether or not a given sound was interpreted as /d/ or /t/ depended upon the character of the vowel that followed it.

Vowels themselves are even more difficult to characterize in terms of their physical characteristics. As noted above, vowels are traditionally identified by their formants. Formants are narrow bands of frequencies, narrow enough to sound something like musical sounds. They are produced by the shape of the mouth-throat cavity. That cavity provides a resonating chamber for the output of the vocal cords. It selects different frequencies to resonate to depending on its shape; therefore, as we change the shape of the mouth we change the frequency of the harmonics that resonate to the output of vocal cords. In general, vowels for particular speakers can be identified with particular formant frequencies. But among different speakers—children, women, as well as different men—it is impossible to characterize any given vowel by the formants that compose it, or by any relation among these formants (Garrett and Fodor, 1968).

The Theory of Grammar

Consider the hapless child trying to learn the sounds of his native language. How can he possibly learn to distinguish among speech sounds by their physical characteristics when carefully trained adults cannot do so under the best of laboratory conditions? In fact, the child does not simply discriminate among the speech sounds he hears. He invents a distinction and then, as a kind of hypothesis, applies that distinction to the signals he hears. If his hypothesis makes order among the signals he hears, he accepts that distinction as part of the language he is to "acquire."

From where do these invented distinctions arise? From a theory of language, or from a universal grammar? A child has as part of his native equipment a device embodying a linguistic theory of a high degree of complexity. That device enables him to perform analyses of the sounds that he hears. By applying the theory he possesses he can form an account of the language he hears in his particular culture. Eventually he learns how to interpret the language of his culture and to use it himself. It is clear that this process is not what we ordinarily mean by learning.

That children must have some inborn capacity for linguistic analysis is astounding, of course, and seems too radical for some psychologists to accept. At times this notion has been misinterpreted; it sometimes has been interpreted to suggest that each child has an inborn capacity for a particular language, or an inborn ability to speak a certain language. The capacity is aroused by the speech of adults, much as certain instinctive acts in young animals are aroused by stimuli provided by their parents. In fact, however, something much more abstract and difficult than language itself is innate. It is something that is best described as a universal grammar or as a device for producing language.

Because a universal grammar is innate, the study of grammar occupies a central position in modern psycholinguistic studies. While meaning, stylistic variations in use of language, and other matters are important, the basic concern of psycholinguistics is the nature of grammar, particularly those aspects of grammar that are universal. Some aspects of grammar are universal for superficial reasons. These are respects in which languages are alike simply as a matter of historical accident or for some other superficial reason. There are, in addition, deep reasons why all languages have basically the same structure, and these are of central importance to the psychology of language.

We can now better understand the introductory sentences of this chapter. Language is a set of sentences. The concept of the sentence itself is defined by a set of grammatical principles which embody and reveal some very general propositions about the theory of language. The nature of these general propositions can best be explained by an analysis of various grammatical rules and kinds of grammars.

A grammar can be regarded as a set of symbols plus some rules for rewriting some of the symbols as other symbols. The fundamental symbol is

$$\longrightarrow .$$

It can simply be interpreted to mean "rewrite as." Thus, a grammar conceivably could (though in practice would not) contain the rule:

$$S \longrightarrow . \quad \textit{The dog chased the cat.} \tag{1}$$

The rule is interpreted to mean "S," which is the symbol for sentence, rewrites as "*The dog chased the cat.*"

The Requirements of a Grammar

Before we consider the kind of grammar that is useful for the description and analysis of natural languages, we shall examine some general properties of grammars (Chomsky and Miller, 1963; Chomsky, 1963). Here are some of the restrictions that must be placed upon grammars of natural languages.

1. **A grammar must generate only sentences.** That is to say, it must not generate sequences or strings of words that are not sentences. Any grammar of English, for example, which generated or permitted the sequence *The the chased cat dog* would not be an acceptable grammar. Less obviously, a grammar that permitted the sentence *Political science examined the professor* would not be acceptable.

2. **A grammar must generate an infinite number of sentences.** We have already commented on the fact that in all human languages an infinite number of sentences is possible.

3. **The grammar must generate that infinite possibility of sentences by applying a finite set of rules to a finite set of symbols.** The set of symbols will include the phonetic elements, the letters, or the vocabulary of the language in which the sentences are written and will include, in addition, a special set of symbols having to do only with the grammar.

4. **The grammar must not allow an arbitrary limit on the length of sentences.** This requirement is really a consequence of (2) and (3) above. If an infinite set of sentences is generated from a finite set of symbols, there must be some means for repeating symbols so that sentences can be indefinitely long. No one has ever uttered an English sentence that is 100,000 words long, but such a sentence is theoretically possible.

The main limitation on actual sentence length is the poor information-processing capacity of human beings. Consider the sentence: "The book that the box that the dog that the boy that you chased owned dug up contained was a first edition." That sentence is not terribly long but it is almost impossible to understand. Yet it is a perfectly *grammatical* English sentence. It is not acceptable because it is stylistically clumsy. Such a sentence is built on a principle of self-embedding. Self-embedding sentences that contain more than two clauses are difficult to understand because it is hard to remember what verb belongs with what subject. But shorter versions of self-embedded sentences are easy to understand. "The book [that] the box contained was a first edition," is a self-embedded sentence with only one clause embedded between the subject and predicate of the main clause. Notice that the element "that" may be suppressed in such sentences.

Each clause in this sentence can stand as a sentence itself with a little rearranging. "The book was a first edition." "The box contained a book." "The dog dug up the box." "The boy owned the dog." "You chased the boy." In the derivation of the original sentence by grammatical rules the symbol S is repeated for each of these clauses that can stand as independent elements. This repetition is called *recursion*, and recursion is necessary to any grammar that must generate an infinite number of sentences from a finite set of symbols.

Necessarily, some sentences must be indefinitely long. The operation of recursion, then, is central to grammatical theory. Restrictions on sentence length are not part of the grammar. Put another way, restrictions on sentence length belong to the performance, not the competence aspect of speech.

Elementary Grammars

In the section that follows we shall examine several different kinds of grammars. Many of these grammars will be strange. They are designed not to generate sequences of words in a real language, but simply to generate more or less arbitrary strings of symbols which have certain properties. For example, consider a language the sentences of which are written with only two symbols. These symbols are "*a*" and "*b*." This particular language is one in which the right half of any given sentence is always the mirror image of the left half. Possible sentences in that language would be: "*aa*," "*bb*," "*baab*," "*aabbaa*," etc.

There is a set of formal rules that will generate all of the sequences that are sentences in this language, and those rules will not generate sequences that are not sentences (see under three Elementary Grammars Compared below). All the sentences of this language will have the mirror-image property. Artificial languages such as this one are interesting because they exhibit many of the general properties of languages and their associated grammars. Some of the properties apply to more important systems, such as the grammars of real languages.

The most elementary kind of grammar is a list. A list grammar takes the form

$$S \longrightarrow a_1; \ldots a_n; \qquad (2)$$

S is the general designation for "sentence," and a_1 through a_n stand for the indefinitely large set of sentences possible in the language. The sentences are "denumberably infinite." That means the set of sentences can correspond, for example, to the set of positive integers.

The grammar has but one rule. That rule says: "Rewrite sentence as a set of particular sentences." Such a grammar is beautifully simple, but it is not very useful. It provides for nothing but a dictionary of possible sentences. Such a dictionary would have to be infinitely big; therefore the idea of a list grammar is absurd. However, several of the theories of language held by older psychologists and linguists implied a kind of list grammar in order to "account for" the ability of people to use language.

A more interesting grammar is one that contains just two rules. It is more interesting because one of its rules is recursive. The rules are

$$S \longrightarrow a \tag{3}$$

$$S \longrightarrow aS \tag{4}$$

The second rule of this grammar (4) is the recursive one. The actual sentences in the language contain but one symbol, a. Therefore the second rule does not define an actual sentence in the language. The S on the right hand side must be rewritten. It can be rewritten by applying either rule (3) or rule (4). If rule (3) is applied, the sentence aa automatically results. If rule (4) is applied, there must be at least one more step in the derivation of the sentence. The derivation of any particular sentence must continue until there are no more symbols of the sort S in the sequence. Eventually rule (3) must apply. That means that the final sequence of symbols must contain only the actual symbols allowed in the sentences of the language.

The sentences defined by this grammar are a, aa, aaa, $aaaa$, etc. To generate the sentence, aaa, the rules would be applied in the following way:

write	S	(step one);	(5)
rewrite S as,	aS	(apply rule 4);	(6)
rewrite aS as	aS, aaS	(reapply rule 4);	(7)
rewrite S as	a, aaa	(apply rule 3, which terminates the derivation).	(8)

Note that the grammar generates a structural description for each sentence. The structural description is the sequence of application of rules (more about this later). Thus, if we have a grammar G, and a language L, we can not only derive all the sentences of L, but also the structural descriptions assigned to particular sentences by G.

Tree Diagrams

There are several equivalent ways of representing the structural descriptions of particular sentences. One is by labeled bracketing. Labeled bracketing is rather like traditional parsing. We shall see some examples of representation by labeled brackets when we deal with problems in the grammar of English. A more widely used way of representing the structure of a sentence is by a tree diagram. Both bracketing and tree diagrams reveal the constituents of sentences. Here is the sentence *aaa*, as defined by rules (3) and (4), represented by means of a tree diagram.

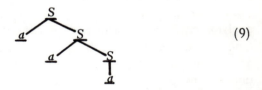

(9)

One starts at the top of a tree and reads down the branches. Thus in (9) one starts with S and branches to *a* and S. The S at the second level branches again into *a* and S. At the third level, S leads only to *a*. The branches always end in symbols of the actual sentences in the language. The sentence itself is simply the terminal branches reading from left to right. The branches depart from nodes, and each node is dominated by the one above it. That is to say, one always starts at the top in constructing or reading such a diagram. The elements below depend upon those above. Since the actual symbols in the sentences of the language are those at the very bottom, they all depend upon the higher elements. That is why one cannot start the analysis of a language by beginning with the level of its phonetic elements. The concept of level is very important in the theory of grammar, and we shall have several occasions to discuss it at length.

Three Elementary Grammars Compared

Let us now consider three alternative grammars (Chomsky, 1956). The reader who is not interested in abstract properties of grammar may skip this section. It is not necessary to the discussion of English grammar which follows.

The following languages, L, illustrate different kinds of grammars, G.

L_1. L_1 contains the sentences *ab, aabb, aaabbb*, etc. These are sentences in which there are *n* occurrences of *a*, followed by the same number of occurrences of *b* and only these.

L_2. L_2 contains *aa, bb, abba, baab, aabbaa*, etc. This is the mirror-image language.

L_3. L_3 contains *aa, bb, abab, baba, aabaab*, etc. All the sentences in this language consist of a string followed again by that identical string.

A grammar, G_1, for L_1 is as follows:

$$S \longrightarrow ab \qquad (10)$$

$$S \longrightarrow aSb \qquad (11)$$

A grammar, G_2 for L_2 is as follows:

$$S \longrightarrow aa \qquad (12)$$

$$S \longrightarrow bb \qquad (13)$$

$$S \longrightarrow aSa \qquad (14)$$

$$S \longrightarrow bSb. \qquad (15)$$

Note that both G_1 and G_2 are self-embedding grammars. That is to say, the recursive element *S* occurs in the middle of symbols that appear in actual sentences in the language. That can be seen in the tree diagram for a sentence in L_2:

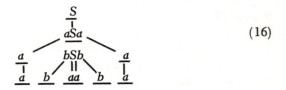

(16)

We have already seen that English is a language that contains self-embedding sentences. Any language that contains self-embedding elements defeats any kind of analysis by stimulus-response chains.

The grammar, G_3, that generates L_3 is a bit more complicated. We can, however, make it simple by introducing more powerful rules than we have discussed thus far. We shall define a new symbol, x, that stands for any string of symbols containing just the terms a and b. We also need a symbol # that defines the beginning and end of sentences. Thus, the grammar of L_3 is as follows:

$$S \longrightarrow aS \tag{17}$$

$$S \longrightarrow bS \tag{18}$$

$$\#xS\# \longrightarrow \#xx\# \tag{19}$$

Rules (17) and (18) above permit the generation of strings of as and bs. Rule (19) repeats any such strings. This grammar is, in contrast to G_1 and G_2, not a self-embedding grammar. There are dependencies in the tree diagram but they do not separate already generated elements the way G_1 and G_2 do.

A Fragment of English Grammar

Now it is time for us to consider a fragment of English grammar developed from the point of view exemplified above. This fragment will show how some of the abstract properties we have been discussing apply to the grammars of real languages. We shall not at this point consider all of the problems inherent in developing a grammar for a natural language. A natural language is something more than an arbitrary string of symbols; it is a system for pairing different strings of symbols (or sounds) with various meanings. The need for such pairing—which is the motivation for natural languages—introduces unique problems that require separate treatment. However, at this point we can sketch out in an informal way some aspects of the application of abstract grammatical principles to English.

The kinds of grammars we have been considering thus far are called *phrase-structure grammars* (Chomsky, 1957). Here is a small phrase-structure grammar for a portion of English (Chomsky and Miller, 1963).

$$S \longrightarrow AB \tag{20}$$
$$A \longrightarrow CD \tag{21}$$
$$B \longrightarrow EA \tag{22}$$
$$C \longrightarrow a, the, another, . \ . \ . \ . \ . \ . \tag{23}$$
$$D \longrightarrow ball, boy, girl, \ . \ . \ . \ . \ . \ . \tag{24}$$
$$E \longrightarrow hit, strike, \qquad . \ . \ . \ . \ . \ . \tag{25}$$

By using these rules we can generate such sentences as *the boy hit the girl*. Here is the derivation of that sentence represented as a tree diagram:

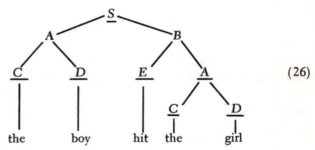

$$(26)$$

The sentence may also be represented by labeled brackets:

$$\#(_S(_A(_C \ the)_C \ (_D \ boy)_D)_A \ (_B(_E \ hit)_E$$

$$(_A(_C \ the)_C \ (_D \ girl)_D)_A)_B)_S\#. \tag{27}$$

Each successive level of nodes in (26) (or each pair of brackets in (27)) defines a level in the grammatical analysis of this sentence. The nodes at each are called *P markers* (for phrase markers). The *P markers* name a particular grammatical structure, such as noun phrase plus verb phrase. Noun phrases can be subjects of sentences, so the A in tree diagram (26) directly under *S* is what traditional grammar describes as the subject of the sentence. *B* is a predicate of the sentence. For reasons that we shall not go into, generative grammars in general dispense with such functional terms as subject and predicate. Therefore, we shall simply label these as noun phrase and verb phrase respectively. Notice that a noun phrase can appear not only as a traditional subject but as part of the traditional predicate. *C* names the lexical class of articles (or, more generally, determiners). *D* names the class of nouns, and *E* that of verbs. Thus, the grammatical rules can be rewritten:

$$\text{SENTENCE} \longrightarrow \text{NOUN PHRASE} + \text{VERB PHRASE} \quad (28)$$
$$\text{NOUN PHRASE} \longrightarrow \text{DETERMINER} + \text{NOUN} \quad (29)$$
$$\text{VERB PHRASE} \longrightarrow \text{VERB} + \text{NOUN PHRASE} \quad (30)$$
$$\text{VERB} \longrightarrow \textit{hit, struck, } \ldots \ldots \ldots \ldots \quad (31)$$
$$\text{NOUN} \longrightarrow \textit{boy, girl, } \ldots \ldots \ldots \ldots \quad (32)$$
$$\text{DETERMINER} \longrightarrow \textit{a, the, } \ldots \ldots \ldots \ldots \quad (33)$$

The symbol $+$ has a special meaning. It names the operation of concatenation. In general, concatenation refers to any arrangement of elements. In algebraic theory the concatenation operation is associative but noncommutative. Thus, $x + (y + z) = (x + y) + z$, and $x + y = x + y$, but not $x = x + y - y$. Aside from such strange symbols and the failure to use functional terms, the grammatical rules read like the ordinary rules of English.

The grammatical terms, such as noun phrase, verb phrase, etc., never appear in actual sentences of the language (save in the special case of talking about language), but they are part of the structure of the language. They are, in general, part of the *deep* structure of the language as opposed to the *surface* structure. The distinction between deep structure and surface structure is an important and highly developed distinction in generative theory. We shall not deal with its technical aspects in any detail. To a first approximation we can say that the deep structure consists of those elements at all the higher nodes in the tree diagram (the *P markers*), while the surface structure consists of the actual string of symbols (words or sounds) in the language. The elements of the deep structure are not, as was once supposed, mere arbitrary conveniences. They are determined by the universal character of grammar.

The six rules for English sentences presented above will generate only a trivial subset of possible English sentences. Furthermore, unless we are careful to spell out the class of verbs and nouns in a very restricted way, the danger arises of generating some sequences that are not good sentences in English. For example, most abstract nouns cannot be subjects for action verbs, such as *hit* (consider *justice hit the girl*). Furthermore, not all verbs are transitive (consider *the boy stood the girl*). Furthermore, obvious matters such as verb, tense, and person are ignored. We shall, by the way, pretty thoroughly ignore these aspects of grammar. They loom large in teaching about language because they are more or less arbitrary features that must be learned, often by rote. In psycholinguistic studies we shall be more concerned with those parts of the grammar that are so important that they are intuitive. Because they are intuitive, we need to make them explicit in grammatical theory.

If we continued to expand and correct that little fragment of English grammar, we would soon run into some nearly insurmountable problems. For example, we might easily generate from a set of rules like that given above the sentence *John felt remorse*. The grammar would also generate *remorse felt John*, which is a very peculiar sentence. The most important reason why the grammar we have given will so easily generate inappropriate sentences is that the rules of phrase structure grammars are context free. The rewrite rules of such grammars are of the form:

$$S \longrightarrow x. \tag{34}$$

There are no restrictions placed upon the occurrence of the rewrite. Under any conditions whatever, we can rewrite S as x. Such grammars, by themselves, are not sufficiently subtle or general to permit accurate derivations of English sentences. The result is that the theory of grammar must be expanded so as to produce a universal grammar capable of handling the structural problems that appear in human languages. The grammars we have been considering thus far are special cases of such a universal grammar. In the next section we shall consider the form such a universal grammar must take (Chomsky, 1965; 1967).

A Universal Grammar for Natural Languages

A universal grammar consists of rules that generate deep structures together with rules that map these into appropriate surface structures. In the most recent versions of generative theory, these are called the *base* and *transformational* components of the grammar respectively. The base component consists of a categorical system and the lexicon (the vocabulary). The categorical system is a phrase-structure grammar of precisely the sort we have been considering. That is to say, it consists of context-free rules of the type of (34) above. However, we shall modify the form these rules take in one minor respect. Instead of allowing the categories *noun, verb*, etc. to be rewritten in this way:

$$\text{NOUN} \longrightarrow \text{boy, girl, ball, . . .,} \tag{35}$$

we shall require that they be rewritten into dummy symbols. Thus:

$$\text{NOUN} \longrightarrow \text{O} \tag{36}$$
$$\text{VERB} \longrightarrow \text{O, etc.} \tag{37}$$

By doing so we can permit the base components of the grammar to remain context free. These dummy symbols are terminal symbols. That is to say, they cannot appear on the left hand side of the arrow in any rewrite rule of the base component. Certain other symbols that have this terminal rewrite-limitation are the familiar "function words" of the language (*of, to, that*, etc.).

In addition to the base-component rules, there are transformational rules. These transformational rules are applied in a cyclic fashion. They are applied first at the highest level (the lowest node in a tree diagram), and they are then applied successively at higher levels until the surface structure is generated. In order to illustrate the limitations in the application of particular words to derived structures, let us consider a particular derivation (Chomsky, 1967, p. 424). The rules are:

$$
\begin{array}{lll}
S & \longrightarrow NP + AUX + VP & (38) \\
VP & \longrightarrow FORM\ OF\ THE\ VERB\ to\ be + ADJECTIVE & (39) \\
VP & \longrightarrow V + (NP) + (of\ NP) & (40) \\
NP & \longrightarrow (DETERMINER) + N + (that\ S) & (41) \\
AUX & \longrightarrow PAST\ TENSE & (42) \\
AUX & \longrightarrow MODAL\ AUXILIARY & (43) \\
N & \longrightarrow O & (44) \\
V & \longrightarrow O & (45) \\
ADJ & \longrightarrow O & (46) \\
DET & \longrightarrow O & (47) \\
MOD\ A & \longrightarrow O & (48)
\end{array}
$$

The parentheses mean that the elements within them may be deleted optionally. The other terms have either the meanings we have assigned them in this chapter or the usual meanings of English. Thus modal auxiliaries are such elements as *will*, *must*, etc.

The categorical (phrase structure) component of this grammar will provide for such derivations as:

$$
\begin{array}{l}
S \hspace{9cm} (49) \\
NP + AUX + VP \\
NP + AUX + V + NP + of + NP \\
DET + N + AUX + V + N + of + DET + N + that + S \\
DET + N + MOD\ A + V + N + of + DET + N + that + S \\
O + O + O + O + O + of + O + O + that + S \\
O + O + O + O + O + of + O + O + that + NP + VP \\
O + O + O + O + O + of + O + O + that + NP + AUX + V \\
O + O + O + O + O + of + O + O + that + N + AUX + V \\
O + O + O + O + O + of + O + O + that + N + past + V \\
O + O + O + O + O + of + O + O + that + O + past + O.
\end{array}
$$

The lexicon is:

NOUN ⟶	*it, fact, John, Bill, boy, future*	(50)
VERB ⟶	*dream, see, persuade, annoy*	(51)
ADJ ⟶	*sad*	(52)
MOD A ⟶	*will*	(53)
DET ⟶	*the.*	(54)

The lexicon specifies the surface structure from the base derivations. Each word in the lexicon is described by certain features. These features are syntactic. They tell us which O (dummy symbol) in the base derivation the word can replace. For example, the verb *hit* is an active, transitive verb that requires an object or animate being as an agent. For convenience a tree diagram completing the derivation of (49) is:

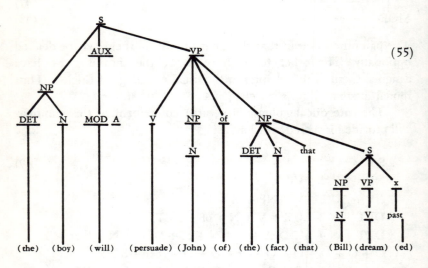

(55)

The selection of the lexicon to match the derivation is severely limited. Thus, of the verbs, only *persuade* can replace an occurrence of O which derives, at its next higher level, from V, when, at that level, the V is followed by NP + *of* + NP. Thus, *persuade John of the fact* makes sense, but *dream John of the fact* does not. The rules for replacing O's by words are clearly context restrictive. That is why they are transformational. We need to know what the appropriate syntactic features for the lexical items are in order to apply the *context-restrictive* rules that apply in replacing the O's with the right words. Context restrictive means that the insertion of any particular lexical item depends upon the nature of the phrase markers. We have to know what kind of construction a particular sentence has before we can insert a given word in a given position. Such knowledge cannot be characterized as being context free. Such knowledge implies that we know something about the P *markers* at deeper levels.

Thus, while the various abstract grammars we introduced in an earlier section contain characteristics that apply to the grammars of natural human languages, they are in a fundamental sense inadequate. They are inadequate because they are entirely context free. The grammars for human languages must contain at least some elements which are context restrictive or context sensitive.

In order to provide a semantic interpretation of the sentence (49), we need both the information in the lexicon and in the derivation (49). That is to say, we need the structure of the categorical component and the lexicon. With that information we can interpret, within a linguistic framework, the sentence *the boy will persuade John of the fact that Bill dreamed*. With that information we still cannot provide a full phonetic interpretation of the sentence. We cannot characterize the phonetic components of the grammar. We can, however, go on to classify each unique sentence in such a way as to distinguish its phonetic structure from that of all other sentences. In order to do that, the phonological component of the grammar must take into account information available in the labeled bracket structure (or the tree diagram). There is a particular way in which this information is applied (Chomsky and Halle, 1968), but at this point we shall not examine the question in detail.

Transformations

We shall now turn our attention to the general question of the nature of transformational rules and how they differ from the phrase-structure rules that define the base component. Transformations are operations in which elements are substituted, deleted, or rearranged. The replacing of dummy elements in (1) by lexical elements is an example of the application of a transformational rule. This replacement is not simply the application of a rewrite rule, because the replacement is limited and depends upon the structure of the phrase in which the substitution takes place. In short, transformations are always structure dependent or context restrictive. A transformational rule which is applied to the last line of a derivation depends upon the nature of the earlier lines. If we include the labeled brackets in the strings that are derived (as in the labeled bracket-representation of *the boy hit the girl* on p. 19) and apply rewrite rules to these symbols, we have developed transformational operations, since the brackets preserve the contextual restrictions (the P *markers*). In fact, this is precisely how the transformational rules that define the phonological aspects of language are applied (Chomsky and Halle, 1968).

It is not the case that the most obvious transformational rules are necessarily the best. Consider an early example of a transformational rule, the passive transformation (Chomsky, 1957). The passive transformation operates on a set of phrase markers:

$$NP_1 + V + NP_2 \tag{56}$$

in such a way as to produce

$$NP_2 + to\ be + V + by + NP_1. \tag{57}$$

In essence, the passive transformation inverts noun phrases, adds the element *by* before the NP_1, and adds a verbal auxiliary (a form of the verb *to be*) before the main verb. The effect is to produce in the surface structure *the girl was hit by the boy* instead of *the boy hit the girl*. While the derivation appears to be reasonable, it, in fact, is unsatisfactory, for it produces the suspicious *John was married by Jill* as well as the satisfactory *Jill married John* (notice that *the preacher married John and Jill* and *John and Jill were married by the preacher* are both satisfactory). Or, even less satisfactory is the pair *the ticket cost a dollar* and *a dollar was cost by the ticket.* Therefore, this method of deriving the passive leads to very unsatisfactory results so far as English is concerned. It makes some passives where there should be none. Instead, Chomsky (1965) has substituted a rule which takes advantage of the fact that verbs readily taking adverbs of manner form the passive, while other verbs do not. Thus, in a more satisfactory grammar a verb can undergo a passive transformation only if among the syntactic features specified in the lexicon is the fact that the verb can appear with adverbs of manner. There is some doubt, however, whether even this rule is sufficient. The point is, that while there seems to be on the surface a fairly simple relation between active and passive sentences, the actual relation in the grammar of English is a complicated and subtle one. The obvious transformation is not the proper one.

Deep Structure and Ambiguity

There is one important property of grammar that comes from the fact that in the derivation of actual sentences in a real language, such as English, we apply not a single transformation but a whole sequence of transformations. The result is profound modification in the phrase markers. Languages are not well organized to keep these modifications separated from one another, with the result that two different deep structures may well produce a single surface structure. The result, of course, is an ambiguous sentence. Consider the sentence *what bothered John was being ignored.* That sentence could be a paraphrase of *that which was bothering John was ignored* or of *John was bothered by being ignored.* Nothing provides better evidence than ambiguity that sentences, like icebergs, have their larger and more significant portions hidden beneath the surface. Ambiguous sentences clearly carry more than their superficial structure indicates.

By the same token, we can find pairs of sentences that on the

surface seem to have similar structures but which, in depth, do not.
Consider the pair:

John is easy to please.	(58)
John is eager to please.	(59)

In nearly all respects, these sentences appear to be structurally the
same. At a superficial level, for example, the sequence of categories
(parts of speech) for both (58) and (59) is:

PROPER NOUN-
VERB TO BE-ADJECTIVE-INFINITIVE VERB   (60)

However, the underlying structures of the two sentences are radically
different. This fact can most readily be seen by considering possible
paraphrases of these sentences. The appropriate paraphrase of (58) is

It is easy to please John.	(61)

But

It is eager to please John	(62)

is not the appropriate paraphrase of (59). It is clear in (59) that
eager somehow modifies *John*. The two adjectives, *easy* and *eager*,
have somewhat different syntactic features, and they do so because
they occur as substitutes for the dummy symbol O in tree structures
having very different derivations.

These examples testify to the need for a deep structure in the
grammar, and they also show us that such a deep structure has a real
psychological counterpart in that aspect of the mind that processes
linguistic information. Ambiguous sentences are both psychologically
and linguistically important, and in later chapters we shall see additional examples of them. It is enough to say at this point that
syntactic ambiguity is a linguistic universal occurring in all languages
of the world, and it is an inevitable result of the mapping of infinitely
many meanings onto linguistic forms.

GRAMMATICALITY AND ACCEPTABILITY

In order to apply generative theory to the analysis of natural languages we must make a distinction between "well-formed" sentences and those that are not. Well-formed sentences are formed according to the grammar of the language. That is to say, they can be produced by a straightforward application of the rules of the grammar. All other sentences are in varying degrees agrammatical. These are also, in a sense, produced by applying the rules of the grammar, but at various points in the applications, deviations from the basic rules have occurred. Well-formed sentences are not necessarily acceptable ones. Long self-embedded sentences (like the ones on p. 13) are rejected as unacceptable by most people even though they are generated strictly according to grammatical principles. The reason is that they are difficult or almost impossible to understand. Thus grammaticality and acceptability are not the same. Sentences that are grammatical are not necessarily acceptable, and furthermore, acceptable sentences are not necessarily completely grammatical. There is, however, some correlation between grammaticality and acceptability, for if sentences depart too far from being well formed, they are nearly always judged to be unacceptable.

Some examples will help explain grammaticality and its role in linguistic theory. Consider the following sentences:

John exhibits sincerity. (63)
Sincerity exhibits John. (64)
Sincerity wins misery. (65)
Sincerity wins the game. (66)
Misery loves company. (67)

Of these sentences, only (63) is strictly grammatical. The others deviate from a well-formed state in that the *syntactic features* associated with the individual words (*sincerity, win, John, misery,* etc.) violate the rules of substitution for the terminal symbols permitted

by the grammar (see pp. 22–24). Not all of these sentences appear
to be strange, however. *Misery loves company* is familiar and would
probably be judged to be perfectly acceptable English by most people.
However, *sincerity wins misery* strikes us as strange. It is not as strange
as *sincerity exhibits John*, for it has a fairly simple interpretation while
sincerity exhibits John does not. We can say that (65) means that
people who are sincere bring misery upon themselves (just as we
interpret *misery loves company* to mean that miserable people like
to share their misery with other people). However, it is very difficult
to place a sensible interpretation upon *sincerity exhibits John*. Sentences which we find difficult to interpret are judged to be unacceptable.

Grammaticality is a purely linguistic concept. It has to do with
the *language* and structures that are part of the underlying competence for language. Sentences that are not grammatical are rigorously
defined as being so simply because they fall outside of the (infinite)
set of sentences that may be generated by the grammar. Acceptability,
on the other hand is purely psychological. The acceptability of sentences is evaluated entirely by the judgments of human beings. Those
judgments are the result of a great many factors. Sentences that
deviate too far from grammaticality are judged to be unacceptable
no matter how simple their interpretations (consider, for example,
who you met is John). In addition, style, interest, clarity, and
aesthetic value also determine acceptability.

Generative theory requires that some sentences in natural,
human languages be agrammatical. That is because human beings
are more than just linguistic productive devices. They possess other
capacities and limitations, and these capacities and limitations influence speech, writing and ability to interpret. Thus, actual linguistic
performance is influenced by things other than linguistic competence. It is important that we keep grammaticality and acceptability
separate, because grammaticality and deviations from it are part of
grammatical theory while acceptability is psychological. They are
related because grammaticality is one of the things that contributes
to the acceptability of sentences. The theory of grammaticality is

complicated (see Chomsky, 1961), and there is no complete agreement among grammatical theorists about how to treat grammatical theory. Most theorists find it necessary to define degrees of grammaticality by assigning different values to deviations occurring at different points in the deep structures of agrammatical sentences.

SOME REMARKS ON PHONOLOGY

Some traditional linguists thought that they should begin the analysis of language with speech sounds. This mistaken belief was the major article of faith in American linguistics of the thirties, forties, and early fifties. Linguists who thought that they began the analysis of language with speech sounds really depended for their analyses on intuitions about grammar, physical data about the nature of sounds and how they are produced by the vocal apparatus, and the "subjective" perception of speech. Even so, their results were not entirely correct, largely because they had no adequate conception of the nature of grammar. They found an impenetrable mystery in the way sounds were combined into meaningful sentences. They did, however, arrive at certain conceptions about the nature of speech sounds which were, in part at least, correct.

One important intuition discovered early in the history of linguistics is that speech is segmented. We perceive speech to be segmented into discrete and separate sounds. That is why we can transcribe speech so readily into an alphabet consisting of discrete items. The traditional name for these segments of speech is the phoneme. One way of describing speech (though not language) is to say that it is a sequence of phonemes. The acoustic stimulus that provides the physical basis for the sequence of phonemes is not segmented. It is completely continuous. So phonemes do not "exist" in the physical signal of speech. The varying combinations of frequencies and intensities that define the physical nature of speech do not divide themselves neatly into identifiable units or segments. But out of the mutable patterns of sounds we hear, we abstract separate speech sounds. A trained linguist or phonetician can hear something of the phonemes of a language with which he is only slightly familiar. He perceives the sounds as discrete. However, to the extent that he is unfamiliar with the surface structure of a particular language, his perception of the phonemes in that language will be inaccurate.

In modern analyses, these individual segmented units of speech

TABLE 1
A Portion of a Distinctive Feature Table
for Selected English Consonants

Phonemes

Features	p	b	t	d	k	g	f	v
Vocalic / Nonvocalic	−	−	−	−	−	−	−	−
Consonantal / Nonconsonantal	+	+	+	+	+	+	+	+
Grave / Acute	+	+	−	−	−		+	+
Tense / Lax	+	−	+	−	+	−	+	−
Continuant / Interrupted	−	−	−	−	−	−	+	+

p	as in pill	k	as in cat
b	as in bill	g	as in get
t	as in tap	f	as in face
d	as in dog	v	as in vase

are said to define a feature matrix (Jakobson and Halle, 1956; Jakobson, Fant and Halle, 1963; Chomsky and Halle, 1968). One variety of a feature matrix for speech sounds is exhibited in Table 1. It lists phonemes of English across the top, and on the side are listed the features or characteristics which compose the phonemes and serve to differentiate among them. The features are binary. That is to say, each takes one of only two values. Voicing is an example of a feature.

Voicing is either + (vocal cords vibrating) or — (vocal cords silent). If you look at the table you will see that the /b/ of *bit* is voiced and the /p/ of *pit* is unvoiced. Furthermore, if you compare the patterns of plusses and minuses for /b/ and /p/, you will see that the two sounds have identical features except for voicing. Voicing is said to be distinctive for this pair of phonemes. Features are sometimes called distinctive features because, in general, each feature must serve to differentiate between at least one phoneme and one other phoneme.

Voicing is distinctive for other pairs of phonemes as well. It is for the pair /ð/ and /θ/. The phoneme /ð/ is the initial sound of *these*, and it is voiced. The phoneme /θ/ is the initial sound of *thin*, and it is identical to /ð/ except that it is not voiced. However /ð/ and /θ/ are not at all like /b/ and /p/. They are distinguished from the bilabial stops (as /b/ and /p/ are called) by several features. They are, for example, continuant (meaning that they are more or less continuing as opposed to abrupt, as in the stops /b/ and /p/).

In addition to the phonemes, of which examples are given in Table 1, there is another important phonetic phenomenon in language. It concerns such special features as stress, juncture, and intonation. In English, for example, we generally distinguish between verbs and nouns of otherwise identical phonemic sequence by stress. For example, consider the noun *pérmit* (as in *I received my pérmit yesterday*) and the verb *permít* (as in *permít me to accompany you*). In the noun the stress is on the first syllable, while in the verb it is on the last syllable. The stress patterns of English are quite regular (as they are in any language), and they may be derived by a set of transformational rules applied in a cyclic fashion (Chomsky and Halle, 1968). In general, the phonetic rules of a language are incorporated into the grammar of the language in as economical a way as possible. In order to establish these economic phonetic principles, however, the general characteristics of a universal grammar must be established. In other words, the general rules come first, and the specific elements, such as speech sounds and their features, are derived from these.

SOME CONCLUDING REMARKS

In this short chapter we have examined some of the aspects of modern grammatical theory and its results. Necessarily, this account has been superficial. Also, we must be aware of the fact that grammatical theory is not fixed or well established. It is in a state of flux. We can be reasonably sure, however, that the major features emphasized in this chapter must remain. In order to explain the nature of human languages, for example, we must take into account the fact that human beings are able to make infinite use of the finite materials available in language. The most obvious way in which this can be accomplished is by supposing that there is some theoretically unlimited recursive feature to human grammar. A considerable portion of this chapter is given over to an account of just how such a recursive feature might work.

Furthermore, the nature of human grammar makes it necessary that we abandon older, poorly structured accounts of how children acquire language. We must assume that children possess innate mechanisms for interpreting the limited, inadequate information in the acoustic stimuli of speech they receive from their environment. The child must have available in some form or another a "theory of language" which enables him to make sense of his linguistic environment. We shall deal with this problem at length later on. We mention it here only to point out the fundamental importance of grammatical studies for psycholinguistics.

2.

LINGUISTIC COMPETENCE AND PERFORMANCE

To give an account of the nature of language is to describe the abstract nature of the competence people have for producing and using language. A theory of language must be concerned with a kind of human ability and therefore is, in that sense, a psychological theory. There are two ways in which a theory of language, like the one presented in the first chapter, functions as a theory of human competence. First of all, such a theory tells us what any theory must contain in order to provide for the characteristics of the human intellectual apparatus. Such a theory must, for example, make provision for the human ability to invent an infinite number of sentences. But more than that, a theory of language can also be a model of the way in which the intellectual apparatus of the human mind goes about the task of generating sentences. Thus, a complete acceptance of the generative theory of language as a psychological theory would lead us to suppose that there must be some sort of a device in the head that corresponds—in a very abstract way, to be sure—with the various aspects of generative theory. A fair number of people regard generative theory to be a description of such a device. These people, mainly psychologists, have performed a number of experiments designed to test the adequacy of generative theory as a particular theory of human cognition. These experiments will provide us with a point of departure for a discussion of the empirical investigation of linguistic competence and performance as well as the adequacy of current theory.

Generative theory, then, is both a model of linguistic competence and a description of the kinds of linguistic ability any model or theory of competence must be prepared to describe. Generative theory is not, of course, a complete theory of human linguistic performance. Other factors, some of them cognitive and some of them emotional or attitudinal, have significant influence upon linguistic performance. There is no available theory which provides a complete and coherent account of linguistic performance. However, even without such a complete and explicit theory of performance, we have enough information about how people use language to tell us what some of the characteristics of such a theory would be. Our account begins with the distinction between surface structure and deep structure together with the experimental evidence on how each is a part of the device that converts thought into speech.

INVESTIGATION OF SURFACE STRUCTURE

The structure of sentences can be divided into two parts, the surface structure and the deep structure. The surface structure is the familiar form of the sentence itself. The deep structure is the portion of the structure to be found only in the derivation of the sentence. The surface structure of the sentence: *The boy hit the ball* can be indicated in the bracketed version as follows:

$$(((The) (boy)) ((hit) ((the) (ball)))). \qquad (68)$$

Almost any casual observation will tell you that people intuitively appreciate and use, in their interpretation of language, the surface structure of sentences as in (68) above. For example, if you ask someone to copy sentences by looking at them with as few glances as possible, that person will, more often than not, copy by phrase units, or those units that correspond to the constituents of the surface structure of sentences. However, it is possible to show that our use of surface structure goes much deeper than such a casual observation can reveal.

A series of unexpectedly interesting experiments demonstrates that fact. In these experiments, people judged the point at which some clicks, superimposed upon tape-recorded sentences, appeared to be located subjectively within those sentences. A number of observations showed that the clicks seemed to be displaced from the point in the sentence at which they actually occurred. It is the manner of the displacement that is of particular interest. In one experiment (Fodor and Bever, 1965) subjects listened to the sentences over one earphone and to the clicks over the other. After each sentence, the subjects wrote the sentence from memory and then indicated, by drawing a slashed line, where in the sentence they thought they heard the click. Each subject listened to twenty-five sentences having one major constituent break each, and five sentences having two major constituent breaks each. A major break is a place in the sentence at which there are two or more brackets. Thus, in sentence (68) above, the major constituent break is between *boy* and *hit*. That break divides the sentence into a noun-phrase and a verb-phrase. There were nine versions of each sentence, each with a click located at a different point. There was always one version with the click located at the major break, and there were four versions with the click to the left of a major break and four versions with the click to the right of the break.

The results of this study showed a large and striking tendency for the perceived location of the click to be displaced in the direction of the major break. In other words, no matter where it was actually located, the click sounded as if it had occurred at the point of the major break in the sentence. Thus, the nonlinguistic click appeared to be assimilated to the surface structure of the sentence and assigned something of the function of a phrase marker. Furthermore, this occurred even when the click was not at the place in the sentence where the phrase marker would have been. This is a perfectly astounding fact if we believe that all of the structure of language is contained in the speech signal.

We saw in the last chapter that the acoustic signal created by speech is not, in fact, sufficient to account for the ordinary interpretations of language. There are rules to which the speech signal must conform if it is to be properly interpreted. Those rules are not available in the speech; they are already in our heads when we hear the speech. In this context it is not surprising that a simple signal superimposed upon speech would also be conformed or distorted to fit the rules of language.

A further experiment (Garrett, Bever, and Fodor, 1966) eliminated the possibility that the clicks were displaced simply to places where there were pauses—any pause rather than those intended to mark the phrase boundaries. In this experiment the clicks were superimposed upon sentences in which identical acoustic signals (the same speech sounds) were given different surface structures by embedding them in different contexts. For example, the sentence fragment, *hope of marrying Anna was surely impractical*, could be given two different surface readings by adding contexts thus:

In her hope of marrying, Anna was surely impractical.
Your hope of marrying Anna was surely impractical.

The common words were acoustically identical, because exactly the same portions of magnetic tape were spliced to each context. The clicks were put in the middle of the words which surrounded the constituent boundaries. The results, obtained from a testing procedure similar to that used in the earlier experiment, showed that the physical properties could not account for the location of the clicks. Exactly the same acoustic signal (the identical sentence fragment spliced into tapes carrying the differing contexts) resulted in the clicks being displaced to different places depending upon the context. It is an additional interesting fact that the click in these experiments was always displaced away from the middle of a word. There is, of course, always a kind of constituent boundary at the beginning and end of words and generally none at all in the middle of words.

Almost any one of a very large number of other observations attests to the reality of the perception of surface-structure boundaries even when there is nothing in the physical speech signals that corresponds to them. The click experiments, however, have a special importance. They show that even when a signal is not linguistic it can be assimilated into the linguistic structure. That is an important fact, for, as we saw in the last chapter, so much of the information that is supposed to be in the acoustic signal of language simply isn't present. Pauses and other markers of phrase and sentence boundaries are often not there. They are often missing, and yet we have no trouble perceiving the boundaries of sentences when we hear those sentences. A careful public speaker—say a radio announcer—will use pauses and other linguistic features to mark word, phrase, and sentence boundaries. He will generally make longer pauses for major constituent breaks and shorter ones for minor breaks. However, that is only when he reads from the script or if he is an especially fluent extemporaneous speaker. Most of us pause, stumble, and misplace emphasis in a grossly uninformative manner. There is even some evidence (see Kjeldergaard, 1969) that we place, in spontaneous speech, the really long pauses in the middle of phrases—between adjectives and the nouns they modify, for example. Nevertheless, we perceive pauses to occur at phrase boundaries and other places at which they should be if they are to conform to well ordered grammatical principles.

INVESTIGATION OF DEEP STRUCTURES

As one might suppose, it is much more difficult to perform experimental studies which probe for the reality of deep structure in human thinking. We cannot, as we can with surface structure, easily point to commonplace observations concerning deep structure, though the existence of completely ambiguous sentences attests to the need for a concept of deep structure and for the psychological reality of something akin to it in human thinking. However, because the deep structure is by definition not manifest in ordinary language, it must be worked with indirectly. Furthermore, some of the earlier psychological experiments on deep structure were motivated by an incorrect view of the notion of grammatical transformation and therefore are not easy to interpret correctly.

Let us begin by looking at an experiment that adapts an interesting technique to the study of linguistic structure in general and to the study of deep structure in particular. The authors of this experiment (Savin and Perchonek, 1965) assumed that in order to operate upon sentences in some reasonable way, we must first reduce those sentences to some of their deep structural components via the application of transformational rules. They further assumed that in order to hold a sentence in memory for even a short period of time, that it must be operated upon in this way. Therefore, they made use of the study of immediate memory span as a technique for investigating the influence of deep structure.

There is, as most students of psychology know, a fixed memory span. It is for the average adult about eight items long. That is to say, the average adult can recall immediately after presentation, about eight unrelated items, such as randomly arranged numbers or randomly selected words. If a person hears many more than eight items, inevitably some items will not be recalled (unless, of course, the items are organized into some kind of structure, such as a sentence). In this experiment the subjects heard a sentence followed by a string of eight unrelated words. The subjects were supposed to recall the sentence (verbatim) and then recall as many words as possible. In order to remember the sentence the subjects would have to forget some of the words. The sentences differed in the complexity of their deep structure, and the investigators assumed that the more complicated sentences would cause more words to be forgotten. Thus, the number of words recalled was an indirect measure of the influence of deep structural complexity upon the immediate memory span.

The results of this experiment showed that the simplest sentence type—active declarative sentences—produced less interference with the recall of words than any other sentence type. The more complicated sentence types, such as questions, passive sentences, sentences with emphatic transformational operations, negative sentences, etc. all produced more interference. In fact, the experiment showed that the degree of interference was directly related to the number of transformational operations required to derive any particular sentence. All in all, this experiment provided most impressive evidence for the view that in order to operate upon sentences in such a way as to understand them, store them in memory, or use them in any way whatever, it is necessary to perform the operations required to derive the sentences. For certainly, of all the operations that could be performed on sentences, holding for immediate memory is the simplest. Furthermore, the results of the experiment by Savin and Perchonek showed that such things as sentence length (a factor of no linguistic importance but conceivably of importance to performance) were much less influential upon the recall of words than deep structure.

These results are persuasive, but they are indirect. It is necessary to infer the effects of the complexity of the deep structure by its influence on another task—remembering the unrelated words. One other experiment (Mehler and Carey, 1967) provides more direct evidence for the influence of deep structure upon the perception of spoken sentences. In this experiment people listened to tape-recorded sentences superimposed upon a white-noise background (a loud hissing sound). It is a well known fact that such a noisy background cuts down the ability of people to perceive speech accurately. The intensity of the noise in this experiment was adjusted just to the level at which the subjects could accurately hear the particular sentences used in the experiment about fifty percent of the time. The experiment compared two kinds of sentences. These sentences differed only in deep structure; their surface structure was identical. Sentences that differ in deep structure only are exemplified by the familiar pair, *John is easy to please* and *John is eager to please*. The actual sentences used by Mehler and Carey in their experiment all began with the phrase, *they are*. For example, compare *they are delightful to embrace* with *they are hesitant to travel*. The surface structure of these sentences is exactly the same, but they differ in deep structure. *They* is the direct object of *embrace* and, in the other sentence, it is the subject of *travel*.

Each subject in this experiment listened to and tried to identify ten sentences superimposed upon the noisy background. In the critical condition, the first nine sentences were all of one deep-structural type while the tenth sentence was of a different type. Thus the subjects were set for a particular syntactic structure. Altering only the deep structure of the tenth sentence made it harder for the subjects to identify it correctly. Here, then, is direct evidence that the ability to hear a sentence accurately depends upon the perception of its deep structure. If a person is set for a deep structure of one type and then hears a sentence having the deep structure of another type, he will not hear the sentence as accurately as if he were correctly prepared. Of course, the subjects in this experiment knew nothing about deep structure and grammatical theory. Yet, the evidence is that they were doing some kind of deep structural analysis upon the sentences they heard. Such analyses are automatic, immediate and not self-conscious.

COMPLEXITY AND KERNELIZATION

It would be nice to assume that all experimental studies of the way in which people treat sentences when they perceive them or use them yielded results that were simple and well in agreement with current linguistic theory. In fact, in reviewing a fairly extensive list of experimental studies on linguistic usage, Garrett and Fodor (1968) describe rules (stated in terms of generative theory) applicable to particular sentences and the difficulties in perception and memory that people experience with those sentences. All experiments agree in showing that people—ordinary people—possess the competence to perform the kinds of operations described by the most sophisticated form of modern linguistic theory. These operations—which constitute the result of generative theory—cannot be accounted for, derived from, or otherwise interpreted within the traditional psychological points of view about intellectual processes. They are particularly difficult for any theory that reduces cognition to associations between elements. Furthermore, generative theory does not, as so many earlier "complex" theories of human thinking did, say simply that the human mind is complicated, subtle, or not to be reduced to simple associations. Linguistic theory shows that the human mind is complicated in very particular ways. However, all this is not to say that modern linguistic theory provides precisely the correct analysis of how people perform linguistic operations.

It is disappointing to find that there is no simple relation between grammatical complexity and psychological difficulty. The success of generative theory has been so great both in providing an account of what the human mind can do with language, and providing a theory of the processes by which that mind could accomplish its linguistic purposes, that we might have hoped that all major problems of the psychology of language would immediately be solved. That, however, is not the case. Perhaps it is that current linguistic theory fails only in particular details—that particular grammatical rules are solved by the mind in a different way than they are by the generative grammarian. Or perhaps the device that generates the structure of sentences uses in part some sort of a semantic system for accomplishing its task. That is a possibility we shall deal with shortly. However, one investigator (Bever, 1968) has proposed that we simply complicate grammatical theory a bit. He proposes to do so by supposing that there is a psychological process of kernelization of sentences.

In an earlier version of transformational theory, Chomsky (1957) made use of a concept of kernel sentences. That concept gave some linguistic priority to simple, active, declarative sentences (sentences of the sort, *The boy hit the ball*). His later, more adequate versions of transformational theory made it clear that simple, active, declarative sentences have no linguistic priority, though they may be derived from deep structures in fewer steps than other kinds of sentences. Therefore, the notion of kernel sentences was, for the most part, abandoned in linguistic theory. No matter how simple such sentences are, they are not the source from which passive sentences, negative sentences, questions, etc., are to be derived. Active sentences and passive sentences are derived by application of the same underlying steps. It is merely that different rules will apply at different places in the derivation of one kind of sentence as opposed to the other.

Even though simple active sentences have no linguistic priority, it is still possible that they may have some kind of psychological priority. Perhaps in the interpretation of complicated sentences we resort to reducing them to sets of simple active sentences, sentences which state the essential propositions of the more complicated forms. Bever suggests that such reduction is a possibility, and he offers as evidence for it some observations on short-term memory. Certain kinds of sentences are remembered a short period of time after being presented, with errors that characteristically do not relate to the deep syntactic structure of those sentences. Bever argues that such is the case because we obey the strategy: "Reduce sentential material to simple declarative sentences." The strategy presumably pays off in short-term memory. It may operate, depending upon the task, either upon the deep structure or the surface structure of the sentences to be remembered.

Bever's suggestion is an interesting one, but there isn't very much evidence for it. There is still plenty of room for doubt as to whether the human mind derives sentences in the same way as does generative theory. For example, in order to describe the grammar of noun-phrases having adjectival modifiers in them, a fairly complicated derivational history is required. Yet adding adjectives to the subject- and predicate-nouns of sentences scarcely makes those sentences more difficult to perceive, to remember, or otherwise to process. There is a discrepancy between generative theory and human ability in this case, and it tends to reinforce the view that generative theory does not provide a complete account of the process in linguistic competence, however well it may describe that competence itself.

Semantic Processing of Syntactic Information

There is always the possibility that at least part of the competence for language described by generative theory is produced by some radically different process. Our ability to produce syntactically well-ordered sentences, for example, may have an important semantic component. Handbooks of grammar, particularly those used in the schools, have strong semantic biases. Sentence structures are usually not taught as the completely abstract systems described in Chapter One, but rather they are described for students in strongly functional terms. And these functional terms are supposed to be "meaningful." Something like a functional analysis of a semantic theory may be operating when we process sentences in our heads. Without any explicit statement of a theory of semantics at this point (see Chapter Four for such a statement), we shall explore the possibility of the semantic processing of syntactic information.

There have not been many comparisons of the role of semantic vs. grammatic processing of syntactic information. One of them (Clark and Clark, 1967) compared the ability of people to remember some sentences that differed in quite subtle ways. Subjects were asked to try to remember two different kinds of sentences in this experiment. One kind is exemplified in the following three sentences:

> *He tooted the horn before he swiped the cabbages.*
> *He tooted the horn and then he swiped the cabbages.*
> *After he tooted the horn he swiped the cabbages.*

The other kind had the structure of these sentences:

> *He swiped the cabbages after he tooted the horn.*
> *He swiped the cabbages but first he tooted the horn.*
> *Before he swiped the cabbages he tooted the horn.*

The two kinds of sentences differ in that the clauses contained in the sentences of the first set are in the same temporal order as the events described by those sentences, while those in the second set are in an order the reverse of the order of the events described. The first event (tooting the horn) is the subject matter of the first clause and the second event (swiping the cabbages) is described in the second clause for the first group of sentences. On the other hand, the second event is first in the second set. Also notice that the last sentence in each set has the dependent clause first rather than second. Dependent clauses more often follow main clauses in English than precede them.

The results of the experiment showed a large and consistent difference in the ability of people to remember the two different kinds of sentences. The set with the clauses in the same order as the events related were better remembered than those with the clauses in the reverse order. What is more, when the sentences were presented with the temporal order of the clauses reversed, they were often changed around in the recall by the subjects to correspond with the order of events. Also, there was a tendency for the subjects always to put the subordinate clause second. This result is what one might expect from the grammatical structure of English, but there is no grammatical reason whatever why the two clauses have to be in the same order as the events. The obvious conclusion is that the events themselves were remembered and that new sentences were invented to fit those events. Thus, the syntax of the original sentences was not remembered as such, but only the semantic information contained in the sentences. The point, then, is that the subordination of one clause by another is not remembered as such. The main features of the sentence are not generated from purely abstract syntactic derivation but are remembered or generated by putting together semantic features. The semantic relations then, in turn, call upon new syntactic structures. We shall have more to say about semantic features in Chapter Four. Suffice it to say here they may not be very different in principle from the markers at the nodal points of grammatical branching trees (see Chapter One), but they do have the character of referring to relationships outside of language. That is to say, semantic features are not purely abstract; they have meaningful relationships with events and things.

Clark and Stafford (1969), in a subsequent study, presented evidence to show that certain syntactic features of verb phrases can be remembered by people in much the same way—that is to say, by the use of semantic features. Therefore it is quite possible that some of the processing of syntactic information that people can do is not performed in a way described by the purely abstract syntactic process of Chapter One, but it may be instead related to aspects of things and events in the world. Meaning is the whole life of language. All else is a cunning and astonishingly complicated system for representing meaning in such a way that it can be transferred from person to person (and perhaps even from person to machine and vice versa). We all know that meaning or semantic information is not bound to the particular syntactic form in which it may occur on some particular occasion. Fillenbaum (1966) reminds us, for example, that people can remember *not open* as *closed* or *dead* as *not alive*. People remember paraphrases, sometimes quite complicated, of sentences, even when those paraphrases have no words in common. All of this suggests that the semantic component is what is retained in long-term memory and that we use that component at least in part to fashion the structure of our sentences when we are forced to recall something.

Performance Factors in Language

By now we have seen that the theory of the preceding chapter provides us with an account of the competence required in order to use language, and with at least one possible abstract description of the process people use in forming sentences in a language. It cannot, however, give us a complete account of the processes by which people invent sentences, for generative theory allows sentences that people never say. And if, by chance, these sentences are said, they are difficult or impossible to understand. That is to say, the competence model described in the last chapter makes highly implausible sentences possible. What is more, the theory does not distinguish between the merely possible and the likely. There is, in short, no place for the familiar, the commonplace, or the cliché in generative theory. Obviously, some "psychological factors" intervene to select certain kinds of sentences as being more likely to be said than others. The conversion of the potential into the actual is achieved by systems that are not, in themselves, linguistic.

We pointed out in the last chapter that people are not likely to say self-embedded sentences which have as many as two relative clauses, though such sentences are perfectly acceptable in the competence model supplied by generative grammar. Certain psychological factors simply make it unlikely that such sentences are said, and these same or other factors make such sentences almost impossible to understand when they do occur. Thus nobody would be likely to say "The dog that the cat that the bird fought chirped at approached the house." And if someone did, it could only be interpreted by someone else on a kind of restricted semantic basis that ignores the underlying syntactic structure. We know that birds chirp and cats don't, and such information makes it possible to interpret the sentence simply because we know the semantic properties of the words it contains. Miller and Isard (1964) showed that these kinds of sentences—long, self-embedded sentences—are difficult to remember. And, of course, they are difficult to understand. Furthermore, one investigator (Stolz, 1967) had only mediocre success in trying to teach people to decode these kinds of sentences by giving instruction about and providing models for their syntactic structure. Because of their syntax, they are simply inherently difficult to understand and to process. It isn't because they contain ideas that are difficult to understand—semantically difficult sentences such as *ideas are green* are quite easy to remember and process. It is simply a matter of getting the information into a form so that it can be processed by the human mind.

Of all of the limitations imposed on linguistic performance by the restricted abilities of the human mind, memory is the most obvious and perhaps the most general. We cannot put together the separated clauses of self-embedded sentences because we cannot hold them all in mind at once—we have, in the jargon of psychology, a limited span of apprehension. We have no way of pairing the particular verbs with their respective nouns, and so there is no syntactic frame into which we can put our understanding of the separate words. Undoubtedly, our abilities both to compose and understand sentences depend upon those sentences falling within some immediate memory-span. If a particular sentences does not fall within an immediate memory-span, that sentence may begin as one thing and end as something else. Since this frequently happens in our spontaneous speech, we must suppose that the limitations of memory are important determiners of actual linguistic performance.

Why are there such limitations? The ability to use and interpret aspects of language that we find very familiar is based on many skills and abilities much more remarkable and in a sense more complicated than that required to derive and use long, self-embedded sentences. So it isn't merely that self-embedded and such other difficult constructions are just "too hard." Rather, our inability to handle such structures provides some indirect evidence for the fact that the human mind is highly specialized for certain aspects of the syntactic structures of human languages. It would be very strange if such specialized ability corresponded precisely to all the logical possibilities of language. The possibility of long, self-embedded sentences is simply a consequence of the more fundamental structures upon which English is designed, and it is one linguistic possibility among many that produces difficulty for the linguistically-adapted mind. We have already seen that one investigator had no luck in teaching people how to disentangle such sentences. Perhaps he (or his subjects) didn't try hard enough, but a more likely possibility is that such analysis is beyond the specific capabilities of the human mind. It can be done, but like the dog which can walk on its hind legs, the person who can disentangle such long sentences must resort to techniques that are essentially alien to the system.

Such a view of the linguistic limitations as well as the linguistic abilities of man depends on the assumption that the fundamental competence responsible for linguistic analysis is innate—at least as innate as the normal canine mode of locomotion is for the dog. We shall consider at greater length the question of the genetic nature of linguistic competence in the next chapter. By now, however, it should be apparent to the reader that those linguists and psychologists who have shown that generative theory describes the linguistic competence possessed by people, view that competence as being native to the species. Each human mind is, by virtue of its structure and the structure of its underlying substrate, specialized for the analysis of the kind of information contained in speech. Not only is English constituted according to the principles specified in Chapter One, but all human languages must be built in much the same way.

SOME CONCLUSIONS

We must start with the fact that the function of language is to convert an infinite number and variety of human thoughts into an infinite number of sentences. Somehow, ideas, conceptions—whether they are linguistic or not—must be mapped onto some well-ordered syntactic system. We first think of something, and then we design a syntactic structure for putting that thought into words. At least, that is how modern psycholinguistic theory seems to view the relations between ideas and words. When the syntactic structure is generated, some semantic features operate to fill the dummy symbols (see Chapter One) which result from the grammatic derivation by cyclic application and reapplication of transformational rules.

Such a picture of linguistic ability is an appealing one, and it is certainly, by an immeasurable distance, the most advanced and broadly useful picture of the relation between language and thought yet conceived. It is, the reader must be aware if he has studied Chapter One carefully, detailed and explicit. Perhaps it is because it is so detailed and so rigorously explicit that it suffers in detail. We have seen, in a brief review of the experimental evidence based upon current notions of linguistic competence, that not all of the details of the theory outlined in Chapter One are supported by the available evidence. The generative theory of grammar serves as a model of the *competence* possessed by human beings, but not necessarily as a model of the *process* in the mind by which that competence is achieved. Or at the very least, we must suppose that as a process model it fails in certain details. Furthermore, some other matters of great importance do not agree with or have not been incorporated into the current versions of generative theory as a theory of the processes in human linguistic competence. For one thing, nearly all investigators of the competence model have assumed, as has been assumed in this chapter, that the various steps in the derivation of an actual sentence occur in a sequential manner. Each step requires the completion of an earlier one. Thus, for example, some experimenters (Miller and McKean, 1964) have measured the time taken to process sentential information on the assumption that the more numerous the grammatical operations required in the processing, the longer the time. However, it is not at all certain, from studies of human information-processing in much simpler situations, that human intellectual operations are sequentially arranged. There is some evidence that such operations often occur in parallel (see Neisser,

1967 for a discussion of the issues in parallel vs. sequential processing).

Finally, simple introspection does not completely match the simplest account of the development of sentences we can derive from modern generative theory. Our ideas are, as often as not, in some kind of linguistic form to begin with. We cannot, then, apply some semantic transformational operations to the dummy symbols after having derived the syntactic structure; we must instead have at least some of the words—perhaps critical ones—before we begin the process of forming a sentence. We may, as children were once allegedly required to do in school, make up sentences using particular words. Only, in the real case of real speech, it must be more than one word that generates a sentence. It must be several words connected by some relation we want to express. In short, there must be a continual movement back and forth between the semantic components and the syntactic components of language.

Therefore, we must not regard the rather idealized picture of the derivation of sentences that we have presented as being anything more than that—an idealized picture. It is certainly more realistic than anything any psychologist or linguist has thought of before, but nearly everyone who looks into the matter in detail and with some serious purpose feels that much of the actual process by which we generate the strings of sentences in real speech is still veiled in mystery. What we know has made it possible to understand well some things about language and how people produce it, but we cannot suppose that anyone presently has much confidence in any particular, explicit (as opposed to loose and general) account of how ideas are put into words.

3.

LINGUISTIC DEVELOPMENT

James VI of Scotland, who later became James I of the United Kingdom, once thought of doing a linguistic experiment, or at least so an old story goes. He wanted to find out what language Adam and Eve talked, or what the original language of mankind was. His idea was to put two babies in the care of a deaf and dumb nursemaid on an uninhabited island off the coast of Scotland. According to his notion, the babies would grow up talking the natural language of mankind. James's bet was that it would be Hebrew.

The story is interesting because it reflects the view that language is innate in the human species. It takes for granted the opinion that we really do not need to be instructed in a language, that the ability to speak—in this case a particular language—is within us at birth. For many years, however, the story appeared to be especially quaint to psychologists because most psychologists were so thoroughly convinced that all linguistic performance was acquired by the application of a few basic principles of conditioning and learning. This attitude was reinforced by views held among at least some linguists who thought that human languages were so radically different from one another as to reflect no common principles of organization. This belief insisted that the forms and structures of particular languages were accidents of time and place.

Once more we have come around to something close to the view that King James apparently took for granted. It is doubtful whether anyone now thinks that any particular language is innate, but generative theory tells us that the human mind contains some powerful and general structures for the analysis of language and that those structures are innate. Furthermore, contemporary analysis of the nature of language shows us that it would be impossible for children to come to learn to talk the languages they do if it were only a matter of the application of simple principles of learning. There is no way at present for conceiving of the ability to separate out and understand those auditory signals that are speech and to reject those that are not speech without supposing that some general, analytic, linguistic structure is part of the human mind. It is not a particular language or even a particular grammar that is innate. It is, instead, an innate theory of grammar that the mind must possess. This theory of grammar allows the child who is beginning to talk to deduce the structure of the language he hears and thus, himself, to come to be able to use that language. An often quoted phrase of Chomsky's (1965) has it that the child possesses a language-acquisition device (sometimes abbreviated LAD). That language-acquisition device enables the child to operate upon the utterances he hears around him in such a way as to be able to produce an implicit grammar for those utterances. That grammar, in turn, enables the child to invent new sentences of his own in the language.

The language-acquisition device is surely not highly developed at birth. We know that the cerebral cortex, the largest and most highly developed portion of the human brain, is not fully matured or functional at birth. It must, however, develop during the first year, for the evidence is that the child begins to understand at least some linguistic rules during the first year. Whether or not the device is fully matured during infancy (the first two years or so) we do not know. We do know that the young child, certainly within three years of birth, accomplishes the perfectly astounding feat of acquiring the essential structure of the speech he hears about him, and begins to invent a grammar—a simplified one to be sure—in order to produce his own sentences. It is literally impossible to see how he could accomplish all this simply by conditioning, discrimination learning, or anything else that calls upon only the general and elementary principles of learning. In order to see the main features of this astonishing feat, we shall, in this chapter, examine some of the basic facts about how children grow in the use of language during the first few years of life.

The Beginning of Language in Infancy and Childhood

There are two sides to language, one receptive and the other reactive or productive. We ought to remember this basic fact as we look at the description of linguistic development. These two aspects are intertwined, especially early in infancy, though now one and then the other must be more important to the future course of the linguistic ability of the child.

On the productive side, babies can produce sounds with their vocal apparatus at birth. These sounds are, of course, cries. Sometime around the sixth or eighth week of life, babies begin to produce a class of sounds unrelated to crying. These are the cooing and mewing noises that parents and other adults find so enjoyable. Neither the cries nor these cooing sounds are genuine precursors of language. For one thing, they cannot be characterized by the feature of speech sounds (see Chapter One); rather, they sound like the animal sounds they are. On the receptive side, newborn babies respond to movement in their environments, and sometime in the second month most babies begin to recognize the human face. About the same time or shortly thereafter, they begin to differentiate among people with whom they are familiar. It is unlikely, however, that at this stage human speech is anything more than a kind of noise to babies, even though it may be the kind of noise to which they innately react in a positive way.

During the first month or so of life, infants perform no articulation movements other than those of opening and closing the mouth, The cooing sounds, however, make use of the tongue as an articulator, and, for this reason, these sounds are probably much closer to being foreshadows of genuine speech than the various cries. There is good evidence, by the way, that the cries of infants are differentiated. Cries upon occasion of pain apparently are distinct from those that arise from hunger. These cries, however, are like the instinctively released actions by which animals communicate with one another. They are not linguistic in the sense that they bear any resemblance to human languages. If they are like the instinctively released actions of animal communication, we must suppose that human mothers react to them instinctively as well.

By the time the child is six months old, cooing sounds become well differentiated. He now makes many varieties of them and it is now possible to describe his vocalizations more or less approximately in the way we describe adult speech sounds. Vowels and consonants emerge and are more or less distinct from one another. Infants repetitively alternate some of the simple, voiced consonants with more or less flat vowels, as in "mamama" or "gagaga." The result is the emergence of clear syllable structure. It is very easy for the adult to hear, in the babbling of infants at this stage, the distinct phonemes of the adult language. However, acquiring all of the phonetic distinctions made by adult speakers of any language is a long and difficult process. Children are still at it when they are ten or eleven years old.

The babbling stage is highly developed in some children, though not in all. If it is developed and prolonged, the babbling acquires the stress and intonation patterns of meaningful speech. The result is that it sounds for all the world like the child is saying sentences in a not quite intelligible language. For most parents, however, this stage is not striking because it is overshadowed by the emergence of the "first word." Most babies will produce clearly recognized words sometimes between twelve and eighteen months. By this age babies are highly socialized, at least in their relations with adults. They recognize and respond to familiar people; they are afraid of strangers, and they show favoritism towards certain individuals. There is every indication that by this stage children can respond to entire patterns of adult speech. They seem to delight in hearing chants, rhymes, and familiar phrases. In short, this is the period at which, beyond any doubt, language becomes instrumental for the child. He is no longer dependent upon instinctive and primitive, nonverbal channels of communication.

There is, for many children, an extended period of time during which they speak in isolated words rather than in phrases and sentences. During this period their total vocabularies may exceed fifty words. Most students of child development have assumed that children use these single words as sentences. Thus, an utterance such as "Daddy" may function for a whole variety of sentences and sentence types that the adult might use. It is as if the child possessed the single syntactic rule:

$$S \longrightarrow W. \tag{70}$$

There is good reason to suppose that such a characterization is an accurate one, for children say the words they know with a variety of intonation and stress patterns. These stress and intonation patterns must be derived from some underlying grammatical structures (see Chomsky and Halle, 1968) that include some abstract notion of sentence. Thus the linguistic device that provides for the generation of sentences is beginning to operate at this period, even though the sentences children actually produce do not exceed one word in length.

Sometime during the second year the child begins to put words together into two- and three-word sentences. Children at this stage of linguistic development have been intensively studied in recent years (Braine, 1963; Brown and Fraser, 1963; Ervin, 1964; McNeill, 1967), with the result that we have a lot of information about these two- and three-word sentences. The two-word sentences in a way are more interesting, and we shall concentrate on these. Here are some examples, culled from a discussion of the matter by McNeill (1967):

Nightnight Mommy.	*Allgone boat.*
More milk.	*Two boot.*
See tractor.	*Pretty fan.*

Note that *nightnight* and *allgone* are treated as one word. That is the way the children in question used them; they never separate the parts. These sentences are of a variety of types. However, there are very few transformational relations that children of this age are able to produce. There is every reason to believe that they understand the longer and more complicated sentences that adults produce, but they must do so by simplifying them in some way. The severe limitations children show in speaking and understanding at this stage are not necessarily the result of limited linguistic competence, however. There is evidence, from deliberate attempts to get children to imitate adult sentences (Brown and Fraser, 1963) that memory span is the most important factor which makes children's early sentences short. Memory span is very short in young children, and when they interpret or produce sentences, they must be able, somehow, to cut down those sentences to fit their very brief memory spans.

The capacity to use the phonological, grammatical, and lexical aspects of language grows all through the childhood years. Arguing mainly from evidence of the effects of brain damage on linguistic abilities, Lenneberg (1967) makes a case for the notion that the primary development of language comes to an end sometime around puberty. That is to say, the mechanism that has made possible the acquisition of a language from nothing, reaches its final development, and further changes in language are entirely a result of learning rather than being primarily dependent upon the maturation of the biological substrate of language. This is the age at which cerebral localization and dominance become firmly established (linguistic functions appear to be bound up with the activity of the left cerebral hemisphere for most people), and it is the time during which the effects of brain damage upon language (aphasia) tend to be permanent rather than temporary. Thus, Lenneberg argues, there is a critical period for the development of language that covers almost the whole of childhood.

At the beginning of this critical period, the growth of language is limited by the immaturity of the central nervous system, and at the end it is limited by an inability of the brain to reorganize its processes—that is to say, by the fact that maturation comes to an end. There is by no means universal agreement with Lenneberg's views, but the evidence that he and others are able to bring to bear on the matter argues very strongly for some termination of primary linguistic development by the time of adolescence. If a person has not acquired the ability to use language effectively by the middle of the second decade of life, he will never acquire it. The histories of children reared in isolation from human contact seem to bear out this opinion.

EARLY GRAMMATICAL DEVELOPMENT

Let us return to the analysis of the two- and three-word sentences that children begin to produce in the second year of life. The term that most often is applied to the speech of children during the toddler and nursery school age is *telegraphic*. Children of this age appear to do what an adult does when he wishes to save money by sending telegrams with the unimportant words omitted. The words that people eliminate from telegrams are articles, prepositions, demonstratives, and the like. If telegrams were charged on a per-morpheme rather than a per-word basis, people would probably eliminate tense markers, plural markers, and the other inflections of words as well. Small children omit all of these from their speech.

Therefore, instead of saying "Daddy, please make me a tower," the toddler says "Make tower," "Make David tower," or even, "Daddy tower." There are few articles, prepositions, and auxiliary verbs in his speech. The phrase *telegraphic language* should not, however, lead us to assume that the child, as does the adult when sending telegrams, is abbreviating well-formed sentences in the language. Instead, the child is generating sentences from base structures by using many fewer rules than if he were an adult. In that sense, *telegraphic language* is not quite an appropriate description for the language of children. Someone else has said that children talk in *base strings*. That is almost certainly not true, but it is true that children's speech, in one sense, is closer to the underlying base structure of the manifest sentences than is the speech of adults. It is closer in the sense that the actual spoken sentences can be derived from some underlying structure with the application of fewer rules. Perhaps the most important point is that the grammar of the speech of very young children is quite different from the grammar of adults, and it is always simpler.

Psychologists, as we have noted, have recently engaged themselves in the intensive study of the speech of children. In some instances these psychologists have recorded every utterance made by some particular child over an extended period of time. The original object of all this recording was to see if it would be possible to discover the grammatical rules that children use in forming sentences. Grammatical theory, however, tells us that this is an extremely difficult and probably impossible task. We can, however, examine various notions about children's grammar in the light of the extensive records that have now been collected. We cannot, by means of this procedure, arrive at a complete and absolutely accurate account of the grammar of children's languages, but we can gain some insight into the general nature of those grammars and how they differ from the grammars of adults.

Two-Class Sentences

The short sentences of children (especially the two- and three-word sentences) seem to consist of two parts of speech joined together by some simple rule. This apparent fact was first discovered by Braine (1963) and he named the two classes *pivot* and *open*. Braine's view about how these classes arise is almost certainly incorrect, but his observation that the short sentences of children seem to divide in this way is a useful one. Pivot words are fewer in number than open words in the vocabularies of children, but they are used more often. The class of pivot words grows very slowly, in contrast to the open class, to which the child adds new items daily and almost hourly. Thus, pivot words resemble grammatical elements such as prepositions, demonstratives, articles, etc., but they do not correspond to any such particular adult categories. For one thing, the pivot class also includes words from such adult classes as adjectives and nouns. For another, the grammar behind the use of pivot words simply does not occur in adult language.

In the sentence "allgone milk," "allgone" is a pivot word. It can be used with a wide variety of other words to form sentences such as "allgone Daddy," "allgone boy," "allgone thunder," "allgone doggie," etc. The open words do not combine freely with one another, so a child would not produce such two-word sentences as "milk doggie" or "boy thunder." Following an account given by McNeill (1967), we might characterize part of the grammar of the language spoken by a child who is saying two- and three-word sentences as follows:

$$S \longrightarrow (P) + NP \tag{71}$$

$$NP \longrightarrow \begin{Bmatrix} (P) + N \\ N + N \end{Bmatrix} \tag{72}$$

$$S \longrightarrow Pred\ P \tag{73}$$

$$Pred\ P \longrightarrow (V) + NP \tag{74}$$

$$NP \longrightarrow \begin{Bmatrix} (P) + N \\ N + N \end{Bmatrix} \tag{75}$$

The elements in parentheses ( ) are optional. All others are required. Applying rules (71) and (72) we could derive the following three word sentence:

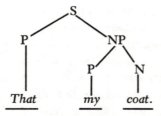

This sentence is actually one given by one of Brown and Bellugi's (1964) young subjects. Here is the derivation of another sentence, also one given by the same subject:

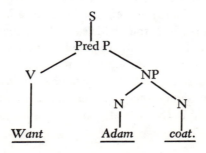

This sentence requires the application of rules (73), (74), and (75). Rule (75) is of course identical with rule (72), so this grammar has really only four rules. In fact, the grammar could derive a good share of the sentence actually spoken by children at this stage. This should give some idea of the severely limited grammatic structure that children use.

As implied by the above fragment of a grammar, other classes develop from the pivot class. These approach the adult classes in composition. Brown and Bellugi (1964) have traced the growth of some of these. For example, the child whom these investigators studied, possessed a pivot class that branched into articles, demonstratives, and an undifferentiated pivot class as he grew older. At a later age, these undifferentiated pivots developed into well-defined classes of adjectives, possessives, and another class of remaining pivots. Over a period of five months, five grammatical classes appeared to emerge from one primitive class of pivots, a class that in itself has no status in the grammar of adult speakers. As the language of children matures into the language of adults, of course, the pivot class as such disappears. Children will no longer say sentences like "that Adam coat." Instead, a child will say "that is Adam's coat," or, more likely, "that's my coat." The major point of this analysis is to show that even though children and adults speak the same language, the generation of sentences is from related but different grammars. In a sense, adults and children speak different dialects of the same language.

Childhood Environment and Early Grammatical Structures

The development of language in children is sensitive to the kind of environment in which those children live. In a later section we shall be concerned with how the child learns from specific environmental stimulation, but for now we are simply concerned with the kind of environment that is necessary for the maturation of language.

For a long time we have known that children who live under institutionalized conditions (such as those found in hospitals and orphanages) during the critical years of infancy and early childhood, are retarded both in linguistic and motor development. Special training for these children later on seems to help make up some but not all of the deficit. The reason for the deficit seems to be that these children simply get less attention than children reared under more usual circumstances. In short, stimulation from adults is necessary for normal linguistic development. However, it is not that children need to hear speech made by adults. Lenneberg (1967) shows that the children of deaf parents who themselves can hear are not retarded in linguistic development, despite the dramatically abnormal linguistic environment in which they live. The quality of their vocalizations is strange, but they are not really retarded in linguistic development. In fact, these children develop into bilinguals of sorts. They are able to communicate with their parents through sign language and with other people by ordinary means. Sign language is not just a code for English, as is for example the telegraphic code, but it is a language having a unique structure of its own.

The most striking cases of unusual environments in which children are found during the years critical for the development of the ability to use language, are related in the various stories of children reared by wolves and other wild animals. There is no clear evidence that these stories accurately represent real situations. The children about whom these stories are told undoubtedly suffered from extreme neglect, but they were also beyond doubt reared by human beings. They are more extremely neglected, however, than institutionalized children. It is not surprising, therefore, that they show gross linguistic deficiencies. In most instances, these cases of extreme child-neglect produce symptoms of severe mental retardation. Few children so thoroughly neglected have lived beyond adolescence, and those who live that long never acquire more than the rudiments of a language. Every so often a case of a child being reared in an attic room (usually out of shame of illegitimacy) comes to light. Such a child is always retarded and particularly so in language.

Thus, by comparing the cases of true neglect with those in which linguistic stimulation is limited, it is fairly certain that it is not just hearing adult talk that prompts the development of language in children; rather, it is the entire pattern of adult care for the child that is important. There is no hard evidence which tells us precisely what components of child-parent interaction are important or what the age limits for the arousal of development by parental stimulation are, but the need for adult stimulation in the growth of normal linguistic function seems to be beyond question.

In this same connection it should be mentioned that there have been a fair number of attempts to teach chimpanzees some form of a human language. Earlier attempts took advantage of the fact that these animals can make sounds that would lead one to believe that they would be capable of most if not all of the vowel and consonant patterns of human speech. However, it soon became obvious that the ability to make ordinary human speech sounds was simply beyond the motor capabilities of these animals. More recent investigators (see, for example, Premack and Schwartz, 1967) have given chimpanzees other systems for exhibiting a command of language. These include various instrumental devices as well as the standard sign language for the deaf. However, to date no success has been reported, and an attitude of skepticism seems to be amply justified. This is despite the fact that certain animals—the dog being the most obvious example—seem to have some extraordinary ability to recognize linguistically formed strings of sounds. It is very probable, for example, that most pet dogs would recognize their names when those names were placed in the middle of a sentence. The ability to do this in any general and extended way implies some kind of competence for the segmenting of strings of phonemes, and, as we have already seen, at least some kind of grammatical analysis is required for such a task (see Chomsky and Halle, 1968).

Therefore, while fully developed linguistic abilities appear to be limited to the human species and seem to require ordinary human experience during childhood to be developed in the normal way, some aspects of linguistic ability may exist in a primitive or somewhat different form in other species. As Chomsky has recently reminded us, Descartes drew upon the gulf that language produces between man and brute as a way of showing that human beings possessed the quality of mind, while animals did not. But the dichotomy may not be so sharp as Descartes believed and perhaps not so sharp as many students of generative theory seem to believe.[1]

The Relation between Adult and Childhood Grammars

Let us return to the grammatical structures of children. The existence of something like the concept of the pivot class tells us that the grammatical categories of children are not the same as those of adults. However, it is also a mistake to assume that the grammatical classes of children are totally unrelated to those of adults. There must be, in fact, some systematic way of getting from the categories of children's grammar to those of adults, for children and adults can understand one another. In short, the categories assigned to the various grammars of children must be such that the potential adult classes can always be derived from them in some orderly way. Put another way, the grammar of children must reflect certain universal principles inherent in the derivation of all sentences.

McNeill (1967) argues, in a line of reasoning derived from Chomsky, that children go through a hierarchy of categories, rather like the hierarchies Chomsky uses in relating grammatically-deviant sentences to sentences that are well formed. The original class of pivot words found in young children serves the broadest possible of functions. A child may make no functional grammatical distinction between "pretty ball," "my ball," and "that ball." Only the crudest distinctions will be evident in any of the sentences of small children, and if we had an adequate way of testing how little children understand adult speech, we should probably find an equally crude categorization of that understanding. Only slowly do children begin to distinguish between different members of a pivot class so as to form new functional classes from what was a broad class. This process must be very like the finer distinctions which adults use when they

---

[1] Recently, R. A. Gardner and B. Gardner of the University of Nevada have reported success in teaching the American sign language for the deaf to an infant chimpanzee. The chimpanzee is reported to have a vocabulary of more than fifty words. However, the crucial matter of concatenation in its use of these words is not definitly decided. If the animal concatenates in some rule-determined way, it will have profound consequence for our interpretation of language. It will certainly spell the end of the Cartesian dichotomy.

distinguish between such sentences as "John plays golf," and such sentences as "golf plays John." A child, with his relatively undeveloped grammatical system, would probably treat both of these sentences as acceptable, but adults, who have more highly developed grammatical categories, accept one and reject the other. The child develops his distinction by inventing rules—in accordance with universal grammatical principles—which account for the speech he hears. These rules make it possible for him to produce acceptable patterns of speech.

Note that the categories themselves must derive from some grammatical structure. That is to say, different classes of words, such as adjectives and nouns, pivots and open words, do not exist by virtue of some arbitrary definition. In short, the child is not free to apply any hypothesis of his choosing to the language he hears. The classes of words that develop can only come out of some universal grammatical structure, such as a phrase-structure grammar. And it is the universal existence of a device capable of generating such a grammar that enables children to derive the functional categories of the various human languages.

Examples of Other Languages

We can assume that the principles of linguistic development discussed thus far apply to other languages as well as to English. There are, however, peculiar features of other languages as well as features peculiar to English, and a brief discussion of comparative linguistic development will be useful.

McNeill (1967; 1968) has gathered samples of speech from two Japanese children who were at a level of development comparable to the English speaking children studied by other investigators. These Japanese children were using two- and three-word sentences. The samples obtained from them included some data on how they come to use a peculiar and rather subtle distinction in Japanese. Japanese contains two suffixes (actually postpositions—in contrast to English prepositions) which serve to mark the grammatical subject of sentences. They are *wa* and *ga*, and they occur as suffixes to the subjects of sentences. They are obligatory, and they have very nearly the same distribution. Any word which can be attached to one of them can be attached to the other. The distinctions in meaning between these two postpositions are many and difficult to convey in English, and we shall not attempt even a rough translation. However, all Japanese adults use them with certainty and consistency.

McNeill argued that these two suffixes should appear early in speech of Japanese children because they occur in nearly all the sentences of adult Japanese. And indeed, they did appear in the speech-samples obtained from his two subjects, although they did not appear in all contexts in which they should have according to the grammar of Japanese adults. Adults use *wa* more frequently than *ga*, but for McNeill's children, the reverse was true. One subject used *ga* a hundred times in eight hours of recorded speech and *wa* only six. The evidence is that the transformational rules that lead to correct use of *ga* are simpler than those that lead to *wa*; therefore, children use *wa* more at an earlier age. However, what is more important, McNeill's children used the distinction between these two elements in the right way despite the fact that the distinction between them never appears in the surface structure of sentences. That is to say, the children had mastered something that occurs only in the deep structure of the language. As a matter of fact, the correct use of these two elements requires some representation of the abstract concept *subject of*. There is every reason to suppose that this concept is a linguistic universal—that it occurs in all languages. Therefore, while the use and interpretation of this distinction itself in Japanese is subtle and peculiar to that language, that use really depends upon the ability of speakers to generate a linguistically universal concept.

Russian provides an interesting contrast with English, for while both languages belong to the same general family, they are quite different in structure. English is a language with relatively little grammatical information presented in inflections and special forms but much more in word order. Russian is a language in which word order is relatively unimportant but in which words are highly inflected. Slobin (1967), in reviewing the evidence on how children come to speak Russian, points out that the early stages of syntactic development in Russian-speaking children look very much like those for English-speaking children. The grammar is grossly simplified, and there is something like a pivot class that goes through successive differentiation. One- two- and three-word sentences appear at comparable ages in the speech of Russian- and English-speaking children. One important feature of the language development of Russian children is that, like development for English-speaking children, the first sentences Russian children produce show fairly rigid word orders. That is despite the fact that word order is much less important in adult Russian than in English. Morphology (the use of inflections) is slow to develop in the speech of Russian children as it is in that of English-speaking children. Slobin argues that there must be something about the natively given theory of language from which children derive hypotheses about the language they learn that favors beginning the production of language with ordered sequences of unmarked classes, irrespective of the kind of language the child hears. Adult Russian speech, as is true of all highly inflected languages, is full of special grammatical markers, but Russian children, in constructing their own sentences based upon the model provided them in the speech of Russian adults, apparently ignore these markers.

The data on comparative linguistic development are still sketchy, but what is available is consistent with the notion that there are some fundamental linguistic universals that appear in about the same sequence and at about the same age in children the world over, no matter what language is spoken. It is, in fact, strong evidence in support of the notion that there is a natively given language-acquisition device that permits all babies the world over to acquire language at about the same time and at the same rate, except for those circumstances in which the environment is too poor to engage the linguistic device.

The Development of More Complicated Grammatical Structures

As the child grows older, he comes to use more of the varied and complicated grammatical structures available in the adult language.

These grow out of his command of simpler structures. For example, the younger child makes negative statements simply by prefixing his two- and three-word sentences by *no*. Bellugi's (1964) examples include "no drop mitten," "no wipe finger," and "no singing song." Interestingly enough, Russian children do very much the same thing (Slobin, 1967). Later, the child is able to produce a greater variety of negative forms. He may, for example, say "don't leave me," or "there is no squirrels." The child comes to use the affirmative auxiliary *do* in order to produce a negative sentence, as for example, "I don't like cereal." The affirmative transformation itself (resulting in "I do like cereal") is rarely heard, but then it is also rarely heard in adult speech. At later stages children mix primitive sentences in which negative elements are simply tacked on, as it were, with sentences requiring elaborate negative transformations. McNeill thinks that the more elaborate transformational structures drive out the others because, in the long run, they are simpler and make it easier for the child to talk the language smoothly and effortlessly. However, this whole matter of the elaboration of complicated sentence structures is so poorly understood that almost any generalization on the matter at this stage is likely to be pure speculation.

One thing is certain. The development of elaborate sentence structures is a necessity. The small child can rely on one-word sentences to a remarkable extent, as can travelers in a foreign country who do not speak the native language. However, such reliance places a terrible burden on the contextual circumstances of the moment to provide an unambiguous interpretation of any given one-word sentence. When the toddler says "milk," it is fairly clear to his mother from the accompanying circumstances that he has spilt his milk and not that he is asking for more or simply naming what he is drinking. However, as vocabulary and the variety of things children want to express increase, reliance on one-word sentences becomes intolerable. One might suppose (as does McNeill) that children shift from a *word* dictionary to a *sentence* dictionary. Children, at an early stage of the two- and three-word sentence development, appear to be using these sentences not in any conformity with a powerful, underlying structure, but rather as a person who does not speak German uses a

German phrase-book. That is to say, he uses whole sentences as words. However, such a use of sentences would soon get to be impossibly complicated—the number of entries in a phrase-book is severely limited, as anyone who has had occasion to use one knows—and there would be motivation to develop generalized structures.

Even so, the notion that the growth of syntactic structures is motivated by some functional purpose does not really seem to be convincing. Rather, from what we know about the maturation of other functions, motor and intellectual, it would seem that the motivation for elaboration of syntactic structures is not so much functional as it is simply the result of internal pressure to do that for which the species is natively adapted. Students of animal behavior find that this kind of idea yields a satisfactory account of the development of instinctive behavior, and there is enough in common between the development of language and various instinctive functions to suggest that the explanation fits here too. In short, irrespective of a "need to communicate," language might simply develop in response to arousal by external stimulation. It may be, in the language of students of animal behavior, released.

Regularization in Children's Language

Finally, in this account of the development of grammar in children, we should examine briefly the well known tendency of children to regularize the language they speak. This regularization is clearly productive, as an experiment by Brown and Berko (1960) shows. They were able to elicit regularization in various ways. They showed pictures to children of a man swinging something around his head, for example, and would say "this is a man who knows how to gling. He glings every day. Today he glings. Yesterday, he _____." Adults usually say "glang" or "glung" after the models provided by "rang" or "swung." Children, however, almost invariably say "glinged."

However, the story is not quite so simple, because children originally use strong verbs correctly. Strong verbs are verbs that change their vowel rather than add the regular inflection in order to produce the past tense in English. In earliest speech, of course, verbs are unmarked for tense, but when marking for past tense occurs, it is almost invariably at first in the form of strong verbs. Thus, the initial past-tense forms for children are often correct. They will say "came" and "went" rather than "comed" and "goed." This is probably a reflection of the fact that such strong verbs are used much more often than the weak verbs (though they are fewer in number), and the young child must hear them frequently in the speech of his parents. But apparently children search for regularities in language, for they soon happen upon the standard forms in English (the *weak* verbs). Then they begin to say "comed" and "goed." Perhaps this is additional evidence for the possibility that the initial sentences of children are little more than extended words without well-formed structure. When the sentences are more elaborately structured, however, they begin to press towards regularization of rule, and the initially correct strong verbs revert to the incorrect but regularized form of the weak verbs.

SPECIAL ENVIRONMENTS IN THE LEARNING OF LANGUAGE

Children, of course, learn particular languages. It is not so easy to say, however, exactly what it is children actually do when they learn languages. From everything that generative theory has to offer modern psychology of language, we know that it is impossible for children to learn particular responses, or generalizations of those responses, as the basis for their linguistic performance. Rather, as we have just seen, recent investigation of language learning shows that what children learn is to choose a narrow set of possibilities defined by innately given linguistic universals. What that narrow set of possibilities will be is determined by what they hear their parents speak.

It is even more complicated than that, however, for it is certain that children must learn some arbitrary relations as well. It is surely for no deep and universal reason that *Pferd* is horse in German and *cheval* is horse in French. Rather, these specific phonetic contours naming a particular concept are arbitrary, even though the internal relations among the phonetic elements are not. All words, in their phonetic shapes, obey deep rules of the structure of language, of course. But, so far as anyone knows, the correspondence between these phonetic contours and particular concepts is arbitrary. Thus, within the limits established by the phonetic rules of a particular language, there is no reason why one set of phonemes should name the concept of *horse* in English. So far as these purely arbitrary relations are concerned, there is no doubt that exposure, deliberate tuition, and practice is that of imitation. Since there are some misconceptions about the role of imitation in the learning of language, it is a topic worth special attention.

Imitation

Imitation occurs when a child copies an example provided him by an adult. Children imitate, at least in the general sense, but imitation does not seem to have quite the role in tuition that tradition accords it. McNeill (1967) presents the following dialogue between a mother and her child:

> Child: Nobody don't like me.
> Mother: No, say, "nobody likes me."
> Child: Nobody don't like me.

This continues through eight repetitions. Finally, after strong emphasis from the mother, the child says: "Oh, nobody don't likes me." It is clear that deliberate tuition with imitation as the tool has failed its purpose here.

Children imitate what they hear, and that imitation is important to the development of their language. However, they do not imitate accurately. In fact, though they use imitation as one of their favorite linguistic games, this imitation is almost always inaccurate. The reason for this is that children cast their imitations within the form of their own grammars. In short, imitation is the hunt for a *model* on which to build a rule or to invent one. It is not the exact copying of something heard. If the imitation by model misses the mark, the child may not even be aware of the fact. All he knows is that he has a rule which enables him to generate an utterance (of course he will not be self consciously aware of the rule). The fact of the matter is that children are not good mimics. They pick up the dialect of their parents and others around them not because they helplessly follow the speech patterns they hear, but because they invent phonetic rules based on the models provided them. Thus children who imitate are doing what the children who responded to neologic verbs in the Brown and Berko experiment did when they provided regular verb endings. According to this view, imitation loses its status as a special process and becomes simply one of the ways in which the child exhibits and expands his rule-forming capacity in language.

Expansion

Some psycholinguists have argued that the parent can and generally does do something more than provide merely a model for the child to imitate. Parents imitate the children's speech but, because parents have a greater command of grammatic structures, they cast children's utterances in adult form. That is, in part, what the mother was trying to do in the dialogue quoted above. More often, however, what the parent does is simply to restate what the child has said without demanding that the child then try to reproduce the parent's version. Since adult grammar is more complicated than the grammar of children, the adult usually provides an expansion of the child's brief utterance. The importance of expansion has been disputed by some students of children's language, but there is no doubt that it occurs.

Brown (1964) first commented upon the phenomenon, and it was he who named it expansion. Since the adult's expansion will demonstrate transformational rules not used by the child, it has the function of showing the child how those rules can be assimilated into his own grammar. That is to say, the function of expansion is not so much correction as it is addition. It is a way for the parent to add to or expand the grammatical structures which children use.

There is only scattered evidence on the effectiveness of expansion in enlarging the grammars of children. We might suppose that better-educated parents and parents having middle-class, school-oriented values would expand children's speech more than parents who do not have these values. There is certainly a difference in rate of linguistic development associated with educational level of parents, and one way of accounting for this difference is by supposing that differential rates of expansion occur. This question of differences among parents in tendency to expand children's speech is related to the whole question of the influence of sociological conditions upon linguistic development, a topic to be examined shortly.

Stimulus Control of Language

A large number of psychologists have made it their main scientific concern to study the way in which reinforcement and various external stimuli control behavior. These psychologists argue that linguistic development is shaped by patterns of reinforcement, contingencies between reinforcement, various linguistic acts, and the stimuli which are the occasions for these acts. They have been able to show that it is possible to change what people say in speech by carefully controlling reinforcement contingencies. For example (see Krasner, 1958), a psychotherapist might be able to control in a very subtle way what a patient talks about by how he nods his head and says "um-hum," after the patient has said something. The patient may not be aware that his verbal behavior is being controlled. It is possible, though few parents have the patience and skill, to teach children to say "please" and "thank you" by reinforcing the children for the right actions and failing to reinforce them when these actions do not occur. All of this concern for the control of behavior has led to something called behavioral engineering, which is used, among other things, in designing specialized training-devices in schools, particularly those in so-called programed learning.

It is sometimes also asserted that selective reinforcement of children's utterances actually changes the underlying character of the language, that children learn to use language because they are reinforced for producing the right verbal behavior. They learn, it is argued, the distinctions in language by a process of discrimination no different in principle from the way in which a pigeon learns to peck at a green light and not peck at a red one. By now we should be aware that this kind of view of how language is learned is seriously deficient. The child discovers what is useful in language—and that includes discovering what kind of verbal behavior leads to reinforcement—by testing hypotheses. The hypotheses that the child tests are not just a random assortment of possible hypotheses about the speech he hears around him; they are determined by a highly developed linguistic system that has a large innate component. Therefore, it is grossly misleading to assert that children learn about language by having their speech shaped by reinforcement. It is possible to change many aspects of speaking by reinforcement, but the important fact is that there are severely restricted limits within which speech may change, and those limits are determined by the things which the language-processing device in the brain can accomplish. The function of reinforcement is to provide the child with some means of testing one or another of the limited set of possibilities he may use in producing and understanding language.

On the other side, the students of verbal behavior are quite correct in their insistence that children will not develop their linguistic capacity to the fullest without appropriate stimulating circumstances, reinforcement, and motivation. Surely some of the motivation is supplied by the intrinsic delight found in doing that for which human beings are especially adapted, but to that basic motivation must be added others if the child is to cope with the linguistic complexities about him. Stimulus and motivational control of language are important, but we shall not deal with them here to any great extent simply because they are not peculiar to language. They play no role in language that they do not play in other things that children acquire, and they offer no special insights into how children come to use language. It is simply that reinforcement provides one effective means of getting people to do what they are supposed to do.

One analysis of speech has led to a kind of classification of language according to its function as instrumental behavior (Skinner, 1957). That classification is often viewed as being a kind of grammar. The analysis characterizes speech segments as *mands, tacts, echoic reactions*, and *autoclitics*. A *mand*, according to this analysis, starts out with a random speech utterance, but it accidentally gets reinforced, just as the rat in an instrumental or operant conditioning experiment is at first accidentally reinforced. The response is strengthened by the reinforcement—that is to say it becomes more probable. The response comes under the joint control of motivation and reinforcement. Thus, a child who first utters a meaningless string of phonemes, is reinforced because the parent hears him say "cookie." Whenever the child wants a cookie, he says that string of phonemes. In this way mands develop. *Tacts* are naming-responses. The child is reinforced for making them, but they do not necessarily satisfy some particular motive. To say the mand of "cookie," the child is supposed to be hungry. But to say "doggie" or "tree," it is only necessary that the child be reinforced in some general way—not in the specific way of having his hunger appeased. *Echoic reactions* are imitations of parental sounds that the parent reinforces. *Autoclitics* are the "grammatical" responses that the parent begins to shape into children's speech by selectively reinforcing grammatically correct utterances.

The analysis makes no grammatical sense at all, and it is not certain that it really makes any sense even in the framework of the analysis of the control of behavior. It is mentioned here because the vocabulary has found its way into accounts of programed instruction and various other aspects of behavioral engineering. However, like the substitution of the neologism *texting* for *reading*, which students of verbal behavior use, this analysis makes no contribution to the understanding of language itself.

Social Class and Linguistic Development

The influence of social variables, such as socioeconomic status, upon linguistic development is important and interesting both for theoretical and practical reasons. It is theoretically important because it demonstrates the role of subtle and inobtrusive conditions in controlling verbal behavior, and it is of great practical concern because

society is interested in seeing that children from poor and intellectually impoverished backgrounds are not economically and in other
ways handicapped throughout life.

Dialects and Social Class

Everyone knows that there are marked differences between dialects
associated with socioeconomic status as well as with nearly every
other demographic variable. The dialect differences associated with
social class are, in many ways, like those among regional dialects. In
fact, class and caste dialects usually grow out of regional dialects.
The most aristocratic pronunciation of American English is found
in the upperclass regional speech of New England and tidewater
Virginia. The late Alfred E. Smith discovered, when he ran for
President in the early days of radio, that the regional dialect of low
status (that of the lower-east-side of Manhattan, in his case) can be
a formidable handicap, no matter how intelligent and learned are
the sentences spoken in that dialect. Smith was one of the first
presidential candidates to speak to the entire nation by radio, and
his low-status dialect undoubtedly helped defeat him.

Some regional dialects are profoundly different from the mythical
"standard" American. It is usually difficult for a person unaccustomed
to the speech of slum dwellers or hill folk from Appalachia to understand these people in ordinary conversation. Jamaica is an English-
speaking country, but the dialect of the peasants is totally
incomprehensible to visitors from the United States, though visitors
have little difficulty understanding urban and middle class Jamaicans.

The traditional view among linguists and sociologists is that
there is nothing intrinsically inferior or superior about any dialect.
In fact, linguists have argued that various substandard dialects are
sometimes grammatically more complicated in important respects
than the standard dialect. However, it is a fact that some dialects are
not socially acceptable. The very fact that we apply the term "substandard" to some dialects implies that these dialects have an inferior
status in society. A person who speaks substandard speech will have a

hard time making his way in any occupation of high status. Further-more, speakers of a substandard version of a language have a harder time being educated, simply because of their dialect. Teachers usually speak the standard dialect, and may not be able to understand the speech of slum dwellers, and slum-dwelling children, in turn, may find the teacher's speech all but incomprehensible. The result is that pub-lic schools, which are supposed to be the great equalizers of oppor-tunity, further perpetuate the inferior status attaching to speakers of substandard dialects.

The situation is certainly bad enough, but it may even be worse than most people recognize, for it is possible that substandard dialects *are* inferior, at least as tools of communication. That, in any event, is the argument advanced by the English sociologist, Basil Bernstein (1961). He has argued, quite persuasively, that socially unacceptable dialects handicap people who speak them for reasons other than the prejudices of those who hear them talk. His point of view is important and worth reviewing.

Bernstein's Formal and Restricted Speech

There are countless studies showing that socioeconomic status and scores on intelligence tests are negatively correlated. Children of low status do badly on such tests, and the older these children get, the worse they do, at least relatively. Furthermore, the correlations with socioeconomic status are much higher for the verbal portions of such tests than for the nonverbal portions. This situation exists every-where, and Bernstein observed it in Great Britain. His data on this matter led him to speculate about why grossly different social environ-ments affect verbal aspects of intelligence more than the nonverbal aspects. No existing theory, Bernstein argued, seemed adequate to explain the magnitude of the differences between social classes in intelligence and the consistently larger difference for verbal com-ponents of intelligence. This state of affairs led Bernstein to a radi-cally different hypothesis.

As any casual observer of the United Kingdom could report, Bernstein found great differences in speech style associated with social class. However, Bernstein found something above and beyond the usual dialect differences between U and non-U speech and between the various regional dialects of Great Britain. He detected two fundamentally different styles of communication; these styles, like the dialects themselves, were built on similar grammatical principles. One of these styles Bernstein labeled *formal* and the other *restricted* or *public*. Formal language is the dominant mode of speech of the middle and upper classes. It is not merely Nancy Mitford's U speech, however; it is fundamentally different from the restricted public style in its logical content and organization. Sentences in the formal style are carefully organized so as to make meaning explicit and clear. The formal style is careful speech, and it is highly structured. It arises in the higher social classes because speech in these classes is a dominant social and perceptual activity. People in these classes play intellectual games with language, and in so doing language becomes *analytic* as well as *descriptive*. The formal style deals with abstractions in intricate detail. By contrast, the speech mode of the lower classes is distinguished by a limited syntax and little effort to make meaning clear. Since communications in these classes are mainly about concrete matters, opinions, and states of feeling, there is little motivation to make meaning clear. The speech style of the lower classes mainly serves for description, and it is difficult to state analytic arguments and abstractions within its limits.

These two modes occur, according to Bernstein, in any society in which there is a sharp division between those individuals who are motivated to communicate ideas and those who regard such activity as marginal and unimportant. The middle and upper class child lives in both worlds, of course. He must communicate with people who know only the public language, and he easily and unconsciously adjusts his speaking to that style when necessary. In fact, nearly everyone can. It is only the caricature of the pedant who carries the formal style into inappropriate circumstances. The young child in the middle and upper classes also learns the formal language. This is a matter of deliberate tuition from parents and the school. The learning of this style is generally supported by his peers, however, for they also must learn the formal style. Abstractions and communications about abstractions are made to be important in the life of the middle class child. The result is that he develops the appreciation for, and the capacity to understand, the formal language. It is the formal style which enables the middle class child to cope easily with the conceptual problems of verbal tests of intelligence.

There are other possible differences between these two styles, some of them suggested by Bernstein and some suggested simply by what we know about the relation between language and psychological processes. We know, for example, that there are characteristic patterns of affect that go along with various stages of cognitive development. It is quite possible that one style is more suitable for the elaboration of certain affective and social relations than the other. We know that affective processes are important in thinking. The work on deprived and institutionalized children makes that clear. It is possible that the degree of expressed feeling between children and adults may be different in different social classes, and this may have something to do with the patterns of linguistic development. These are all matters of importance, but they have scarcely been touched upon in psycholinguistic research.

Bernstein's ideas are related to the notion of linguistic relativism (see Chapter Five). But unlike the extreme position some people have taken on the question of linguistic relativism, Bernstein does not assert that it is impossible to make linguistic distinctions in one style that one can make in the other. He argues only that it is easier to do so and at the same time communicate one's ideas with accuracy. Bernstein does not speculate on the reversibility of the styles one learns in childhood. We know that so much of linguistic development depends upon maturation and experience at the right time, that we may well wonder whether a person in late adolescence, suddenly faced with learning the formal style, could actually do so. There is no answer to that question, for, in fact, beyond the data on obvious social class differences in intelligence and verbal skills, there is little concrete information by which to judge the correctness of Bernstein's views. They have influenced research on the sociology of language, but it is too early to tell whether Bernstein's position is substantially correct or whether he exaggerates the possible stylistic differences.

One thing is probably true. It is probably the case that two separate and distinct styles do not exist in any language. Rather there are *gradations* of style which can be characterized by the two extremes of a concrete, descriptive style and an abstract, analytic style on the other hand.

SOME CONCLUDING REMARKS

This short review of linguistic development has examined most of the important problems concerning how children come to use language. The major point has been that children possess intrinsic abilities to perform grammatical analyses of the language they hear, and to derive sentences of their own using a grammar similar to that in the language of their environment. The grammar of children's language is not the grammar of adult language, but it is related to the grammar of the adult language, probably through a kind of hierarchy of categories. Children learn to do particular things, to be sure, but what they do in language is at the bottom limited by the constraints imposed by the language-generating device they possess. It is the investigation of the nature of this device that is the fundamental problem in the study of linguistic development, not the application of principles of learning, concept formation or any of the more familiar psychological problems.

4.

MEANING

The purpose of grammar is to provide a system of rules through which an infinite variety of meanings may be expressed as an infinite variety of sentences in some language. This proposition makes grammar central to language. It also makes it clear that the grammatical structure of language functions only in the interest of something else. In itself, the study of grammar would be only a kind of idle game, or perhaps an obscure branch of mathematics. It derives its humanistic importance because of the function it serves. It is a powerful and very general device for converting ideas into sentences. It has the function of making communication and organized, abstract thinking possible. The content of language resides both in ideas and in sentences. The content must exist prior to and outside of the sentences of language, or those sentences would make no sense. The relation between ideas and sentences provides the main problem of psycholinguistics. It is the problem of meaning.

The psychological study of meaning is broad. The concept of meaning is meant to describe the content of all ideas that can be expressed or interpreted linguistically. Not all students of meaning are interested in so broad a conception, however. Linguists, for example, are seldom concerned with the nature of the ideas which give rise to sentences. Their interest begins with the sentence itself. They are only concerned with the linguistic relations that characterize sentences and their parts. Linguists interest themselves in such problems as how one can express equivalences among words and sentences (the problem of synonymity), with determining the components of meaning, with the problem of semantic ambiguity, and with other matters that do not go beyond the body of language itself. Linguists, as a rule, are not interested in the question of reference. Reference is concerned with the relation between linguistic events and events in nature. Philosophers are concerned with reference, because they are interested in theories of knowledge, the nature of truth, and other matters that transcend purely linguistic questions. Some but not all philosophers are interested in the nature of the mental events behind meaning and reference. The psychologist who is concerned with language is interested in all of these matters, for his problems are in the ideas behind language, language itself, and the uses of language, as in reference. The psychologist's attention is centered, however, on the nature of the ideas behind the use of words and in the nature of the device in the head that gives rise to those ideas. The primary way in which we know about those ideas is in their manifestation in language. Therefore, the easiest way to begin an account of the psychology of meaning is to begin with the linguistic study of meaning.

LINGUISTIC MEANING

The study of meaning in language is generally known as *semantics*, and it is usually said to be concerned with the signification of language. This means that semantics concerns itself with the problem of what linguistic elements are said to be signs of. The analysis of signification takes the form of describing the concepts which constitute linguistic signs. Since these concepts are in a linguistic form themselves, the concern of semantics is really with the *meaningful relations between words, sentences, and other linguistic entities.*

For the most part, linguists agree that the phonetic elements of language, the phonemes in traditional linguistic analysis, have no meaning in themselves. There is some slight evidence for a weak kind of phonetic symbolism. Phonetic symbolism is said to occur when particular speech sounds, such as the /z/ of *buzz* are asserted to have a kind of meaning of their own, either determined by their associations with things (the sound made by bee's wings, for example), or because of some innate predisposition of the mind to perceive those phonetic elements in a particular way. These effects are minor, however, and it is clear that the separate sounds, or random concatenations of sounds in language have little or no meaning. Syllables, unless they happen also to be words, also have no meaning. In traditional linguistic analysis, the smallest unit of language said to have meaning is the morpheme. The morpheme is the smallest linguistic segment that has a clear linguistic interpretation devoid of context. Interpretation of a particular morpheme without context will not be the same as its interpretation in a particular sentence, but at least it is possible to list the interpretations of morphemes in a kind of dictionary. Some morphemes are words, as for example, *hat*, *nephew*, or *apricot*. Others, such as *saw* (the verb) and *fungicide* consist of two or more morphemes. *Saw*, for example, consists of the verb *to see* together with a marker for past tense (the vowel change). Morphemic analysis was an absorbing interest to an older generation of linguists. The modern approach to linguistics, which makes the analysis of language dependent upon the notion of sentence, does not make so much of a point about finding the smallest unit of meaning. Rather, the emphasis is simply upon any segment of language that can be interpreted. And, we may simply accept that there are segments of language that can be interpreted by speakers of the language in an unequivocal way and that there are other segments, usually smaller ones such as syllables and phonemes, that cannot, in the general case, be so interpreted.

The interpretation of sentences rests upon the syntactic structures of those sentences plus the meaning of the separate elements of the sentences. Thus, the meaning of a sentence may be said to be the meaning of the subject of the sentence plus the meaning of the predicate, plus the syntactic form of the relation between the subject and the predicate. The meaning of the subject, in turn, may be said to be its syntactic form plus the meaning of its separate constituents. Or we may go directly from the sentence to words, in which case we say that the meaning of the sentence is the syntactic form of the sentence plus the meaning of the words which compose it. Of course, in any real segment of language, the meaning of a sentence will depend upon its context. That is, a sentence will mean one thing when buried in one paragraph and another thing when standing alone. Or it will mean one thing when one person says it and something quite different when another person says it. However, these contextual relations of sentences to the language as a whole, or to nonlinguistic circumstances, quite elude the techniques of the linguists, and as a result linguists are inclined to dismiss them as being of little theoretical importance. They are important to psychologists, and they will be under consideration when we investigate psychological meaning.

In general, then, the linguist separates the interpretation of a sentence into a syntactic component and a semantic component. The semantic component, for the most part, is concerned with the meaning of individual words. In theory, one ought to be able to arrive automatically at an interpretation (though usually more than one, because sentences are almost inherently ambiguous) for a given sentence by combining its syntactic structure with the meanings of the separate lexical elements in a particular way. The complete specification of the possible interpretations of sentences is one of the goals of semantic studies in linguistics.

Linguists describe the meaning of the separate lexical elements by describing their components of meaning. Anthropologists have labeled this kind of description, *componential analysis,* and while anthropologists often mean something different in practice from what linguists do, the term can apply equally to the semantic studies of linguists. There is no one way to go about doing a componential analysis. It all depends upon what one regards as components and what formal method of analysis is applied. Often different methods are equivalent or achieve equivalent results, and the choice of one or another, from a linguistic point of view, is determined by ease and by conciseness. Two generally applicable methods for doing componential analysis are of particular importance to the psychological study of meaning. We shall review these in some detail.

Branching Trees and Classification Systems

One important way to characterize the components of meaning of some particular group of concepts is to make use of the labeling system which can be attached to a branching tree or classification hierarchy. Such a system is homologous to a phrase-structure grammar and, in general, has much the same properties. Its use, however, in semantic and conceptual analyses is very different. Consider the example of a classification tree in Figure 2. Those who are familiar

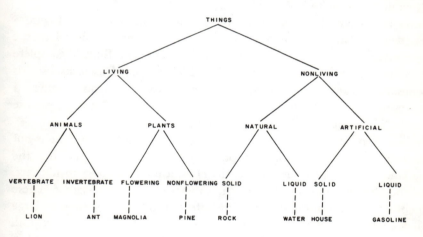

FIGURE 2.
A Possible Classification Tree for Some Concepts Described by Ordinary English Words.

with computer programing will know that this kind of structure is in the form of a list. It shows the relation between a whole collection of concepts. The branches of the tree are labeled nodes or markers. In general, any node is composed of the attributes named by all the labeled nodes above it. Thus *man* is *vertebrate, animal,* and *living*. The particular tree exhibited in Figure 2 appears to include a whimsical choice of labeled nodes. Certain things one would think should be in this tree are not there. This spots a difficulty with any general list or classificatory structure. It either must be restricted to a very limited domain or be enormous. Two of the most widely used classification systems provide an example of each extreme. The Linnean classification system for biological relations is a branching tree defining identifying characteristics for the limited domain of plants and animals. Even so it is enormous. The classification of knowledge used by Peter Mark Roget, the 19th century English physician who invented the *Thesaurus,* provides an example of a scheme that attempts to be very nearly universal.

Figure 3 shows a limited portion of Roget's scheme. The complete scheme is the table of contents and the entries of any *Thesaurus* built according to Roget's plan.

It is obvious that the system is a cumbersome one. Also, Figure 3 suggests that the system is neither very germane nor useful to the concepts it attempts to specify. An inspection of Roget's complete system confirms this suspicion. The body of the *Thesaurus* itself is useful because it groups synonyms and near synonyms together, a result that could be achieved in a number of ways. Most people use the *Thesaurus* as a kind of synonym dictionary.

Another example of a very large domain in a list structure is not a semantic system, though in principle it is identical to one. It is the kind of system that is used in the classification of books in libraries, the Dewey decimal system or the Library of Congress system. These library classification systems illustrate one difficulty with very large branching trees. They must be redundant and/or weakly hierarchical. A given book, for example this one, may fall in between two widely separated fields of study. Or, a given labeled marker in a semantic tree may have to be entered at two different points. Suppose, in Figure 2, we had a node for *mammal* and also wanted to place a node indicating *bi-pedaled gait.* We should have to enter the *bi-pedal* node under *mammal* for *man* and under *nonmammal* for other animals, *birds* for example. It is clear that any improvement on Roget's system or on existing library classification systems would not be able to eliminate redundancies from the system. Apparently the way in

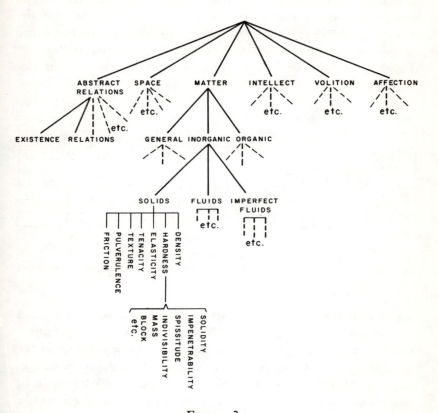

FIGURE 3.
A Classification Tree Based Upon a Portion of the *Thesaurus* Devised
by Peter Mark Roget.

which we want to organize knowledge leads inherently to redundancies, and any attempt to eliminate them would lead to a conceptual system that would be unrecognizable in any language.

Distinctive Feature or Attribute Systems

An alternative way to characterize the components of meaning is in
a distinctive feature table. Such a table forms a matrix in which the

rows are semantic markers, attributes, features, or labels (the termi-
nology varies in a generally unsystematic way) and the columns are
concepts or words to be defined. Figure 4 shows an example of a distinctive feature table which summarizes the same data as those in
Figure 2. In this table each pair of nodes from the tree is entered as

+	−	LION	ANT	MAGNOLIA	PINE	ROCK	WATER	HOUSE	GASOLINE
LIVING	NONLIVING	+	+	+	+	−	−	−	−
ANIMALS	PLANTS	+	+	−	−				
VERTEBRATE	INVERTEBRATE	+	−						
FLOWERING	NONFLOWERING			+	−				
NATURAL	ARTIFICIAL					+	+	−	−
SOLID	LIQUID					+	−	+	−

FIGURE 4.
A Distinctive Feature Table for the Concepts Presented in Tree Form
in Figure 2.

a plus or minus value on some attribute or feature, while the items
to be defined are entered in the columns. Figure 4 does not illustrate
the fact, but nevertheless there is nothing to prevent values of the
attributes from also occurring as concepts to be defined. In fact, in
any "complete" account of a lexicon, each value would have to be
entered as a concept, and in order for every possible distinction to be
made, there would have to be some columns that had only one plus
or one minus in them. These would be the "fundamental attributes"
of the system. The words "complete" and "fundamental attributes"
are put in quotations because, as we shall see later, an exhaustive
semantic componential system for any lexicon is impossible. However,
it is perfectly possible for the feature *animal-plant* to have its values
on the attributes *living-nonliving, natural-artificial,* etc.

Trees and matrices are completely translatable, but matrices are
redundant. That is to say, if the data from a tree are entered into a
matrix, the matrix must be redundant. The hierarchical form of a
tree can be approximated in a matrix in which the most general

marker or attribute is listed at the top and the least general (the ones that distinguish between single pairs of concepts) at the bottom.

Semantic feature tables are less common in ordinary experience than lists or trees, but they do occur. For example, statistical summaries of the graduation requirements of American colleges and universities are often in this form. Each requirement is listed as a feature, and the individual institutions are listed as concepts. Thus, if a given institution requires a year of English writing, that fact would be entered as a plus in the column for that institution. However, feature tables do not require plus or minus entries, any more than trees require that there be only two branches at each node. Numbers or any other code may be entered by suitably altering the form of the rows. Thus, we can imagine a given marker as being a scale, with numbers graded say from *good* to *bad* or *weak* to *strong*. However, there is something psychologically and linguistically compelling about the plus-minus form of the feature table. It incorporates the concept of antonymy, or at least it can, and we feel this concept to be important both linguistically and psychologically.

The Limitations of Trees and Tables

We have already hinted that trees and tables have limited utility. We have seen that Roget's system is disappointing, and that something as well organized as the Linnean system of classification is redundant or weakly hierarchical. However, we might suppose that at least theoretically, a complete and well organized tree or table could be invented for the lexicon of any language. Unfortunately that is not true. The reason is that semantic markers or attributes are easy to invent. We are used to characterizing everything in the universe as living or nonliving, and we somehow accept it as a fundamental given. There are literally endless numbers of other ways in which we could characterize everything in the universe. We could, for example, divide everything in the world into those things that are in Spitzbergen and those that are not. Or, along with the lady of William James's acquaintance, we can characterize everything as thick or thin. These latter attributes appear to be more arbitrary than the division into living and nonliving, but they really are not, for there is no rigorous way to separate those attributes that are "arbitrary" from those that are not. It is only that some markers or attributes are more important than others. Or, alternatively, the characteristic forms of the markers for trees do not contain all possible markers. Put another way, the lexicon of any given language is incomplete. There is no simple name in English, for example, for things that are carried by hand (would manuportable be an acceptable invention?), or the various surfaces of the head considered together (a collective name for the forehead, cheeks, chin, etc.). In fact any semantic feature table or any conceptual tree must either be incomplete or infinite.

This is an important point psychologically, for we cannot imagine that the device in the head that performs the semantic functions of interpretation of language does so by operating upon an analog to an extended feature table or branching tree. We can do too many things in interpretation for that to be a possibility. The author once had the notion that all concepts in any language could be characterized by a feature table having approximately fifty rows (see Deese, 1964). The result would be a possible maximum of "thinkable" concepts of 2^{50}. The number 2^{50} is a very large number—it must be close to the number of fundamental particles in the universe—but it is still not large enough. The plain fact is that features, like sentences, are infinite in number, and in order to characterize the brain's semantic processing device, we must imagine a device with a finite number of fundamental parts that can, in essence, be capable of generating an indefinitely extended feature table. In order to suggest the possible forms such a device may take, we need to consider the psychological aspects of meaning.

Psychological Meaning

Older conceptions of the structure of psychological meaning, like the older concepts of how people process grammatical information, tended to be built upon the various elementary principles of learning. Hence, if one examines this literature (see Osgood, 1953) one finds frequent reference to principles of conditioning, association, mediation, and the like. Considerations like those that have entered into our earlier discussions would make us wary of the application of these kinds of notions to the psychology of meaning. We should be even more wary given what we have just seen, that semantic features can be invented endlessly. However, there are a variety of psychological notions as well as techniques of measurement that do provide information about the nature of the semantic processes of the mind.

Understanding

The basic problem in the psychology of semantics is how we understand segments of language. The test of understanding of a linguistic segment is some response to that segment, usually a paraphrase, which indicates that the essential message has been received. In general, such response depends upon interpretation. Interpretation arises when there is understanding. Understanding is not a linguistic concept, it is psychological. In its most basic sense it refers to an introspectively found feeling of knowing that we grasp something. Human beings are able to sense when they understand, and they may communicate to others this understanding by some interpretation.

The function of understanding is to signal the potential for interpretation. Part of the ability to interpret is provided by the kind of syntactic devices we have examined, but some of that ability goes deeper. There are nonlinguistic aspects to interpretation, of which the most obvious is imagery. However, to say that we understand does not mean to imply that we operate upon each segment of a linguistic sequence so as to produce a series of ideas and images, each of which, in some way, corresponds to a portion of that sequence. Many psychologists and philosophers have taken this view, but it has proven to be a sterile and inappropriate notion, whether embodied in a mentalistic (as in classical associationism) or behavioristic (as in much modern psychological work) theory. Understanding only tells us that we can produce the appropriate imagery, linguistic operations, and other cognitive activity necessary for interpretation.

The relation between understanding and interpretation is a

loose one. Sometimes we read or hear something that we think we do not understand, and yet, to our surprise, we may produce an acceptable paraphrase of it. On the other hand, we may think that we understand something and then stumble when we have to interpret it. Then we also misapprehend, in which case our interpretations are, from someone else's point of view, incorrect. However, we do understand in the case of misapprehension; it is only that we understand the wrong thing or understand in some illogical way.

Whatever the process that occurs when we understand, it is essential to meaning. There are several ways to characterize the process. One is to say that it is the matching of some information to categories of the mind. Part of that process must be the assigning of information to semantic categories. Semantic categories are simply the ways in which we can think of concepts. There must be a large number of them, but not necessarily an unlimited number. In a discussion of componential analysis, we have already examined two processes that reveal different semantic structures at work. They are, in linguistic theory, characterized as branching trees and distinctive features. But there are other semantic categories, some of which are nonlinguistic. It is likely that some such categories are better adapted to the limitations of the human mind than others. Certainly we ought to expect that there are some universal semantic categories. These should be comparable to the universal syntactic categories. That is to say, they should, in some way, be innate to the human mind. All that can be done here is to list some possible choices for universal semantic structures and see how well, with the limited information available to us, they seem to hold up to the criteria of universality. Those choices we have elected to discuss are those with the greatest promise for such universality.

Some Semantic Categories

Semantic categories arise out of cognitive operations, and they are best characterized by the nature of those operations. One fundamental set of operations is that of grouping and distinguishing. These operations require the kind of information present in a feature table.

Grouping depends upon seeing certain resemblances among the columns of such a table (the concepts), while distinguishing between pairs of concepts depends upon finding some particular row for which the feature entry in the appropriate columns will be different. We can imagine all operations of this sort to correspond, in some abstract way, to operations upon a feature-table. Consider the matrix in Figure 3. We can judge any two columns in this matrix to be similar to one another according to the number of like-valued entries they share. Such a process corresponds to a mathematical treatment in which the two concepts are said to project vectors in a semantic space having the number of dimensions corresponding to the rows of the matrix. To the extent that two concepts are similar to one another they will project vectors in neighboring regions of the space. This mathematical analogy is not idle, for there are mathematical treatments which enable us, from judgments of similarity, to arrive at such abstract representations of the way in which people relate concepts within a limited domain. These techniques are called multidimensional scaling, and various investigators of psychological semantics have applied them to the study of semantic fields. In order to avoid the problem of an indefinitely extended matrix, the semantic fields must be limited in scope before such techniques will work. Only in that way can an equivalent to a limited feature table be projected.

Henley (1968) has applied the techniques of multidimensional scaling to the study of how people think about the concepts represented by familiar animals. Her results show that ordinary college students think of animals not so much as being arranged in some biological classification system as in sharing certain commonplace attributes. For example, the most potent attributes these students have for grouping animals are size and ferocity. The vectors of similarity among animal concepts are arrived at by weighting in some way the most important or salient dimensions (see Johnson, 1968). The attributes that apparently are most significant to college students in grouping and distinguishing among their concepts of animals are size and ferocity. Thus, big animals, such as the elephant, the horse, and the camel, are contrasted with small animals like the mouse, the rat, and the chipmunk. Fierce animals like the lion and the tiger (also large) are contrasted with tame animals like the (small) rabbit and the (big) cow.

Judging things to be similar, forming analogies and other cognitive activities that review the basic process of grouping at work, tend to reveal the importance of dimensions. The process of distinguishing —which we have seen corresponds to searching through a feature matrix for a single feature that will distinguish between pairs of concepts—does not reveal the importance of attributes. Thus, if we were to ask someone how an elephant and a mouse differed, nearly everyone would say in size. But, most college students, when asked how a lion and cow are alike, and how these animals differ from a robin, will say that the lion and cow are both mammals while the robin is a bird. While there is no logical reason why people couldn't say that the lion and cow are both large and the robin small, they tend not to. When the question is put in this form, a typical, reasonably educated person will not tell you that animals share attributes in common, he will tell you that they can be classified in some common way. Notice that the "meaning" of the classification may well escape him. Most college students know that man, apes, and monkeys are all members of the primate order, but very few students could recite the defining characteristics of that biological order.

The operation of classification is superordination and subordination, and it corresponds to finding the constituents in a phrase-structure grammar. As in the case with complicated grammatical phrase structures, very large classification trees are difficult to manage. It is an extraordinarily demanding task to comprehend in one grasp the full biological classification system from the top all the way down to the genus level. There are approximately (it depends upon the particular version of the system one employs) seven or eight levels in the standard biological tree. Such a system must, in part at least, be committed to memory by rote, and therefore it has, at best, an ambiguous status in understanding. It hardly seems possible that anything more than a limited portion of an extended branching tree structure could be dealt with by an individual at the time he is thinking about some particular concept. What he does have is the ability to move about in local regions of a branching tree by applying superordination and subordination operations first here and then there.

These two systems, as we have already seen, play a useful role in linguistic theory, and they tend to provide the major components of formal definitions given for linguistic purposes. We must not suppose, however, that people carry around in their heads general and extended feature matrices or tree diagrams. It is rather that people are intellectually equipped to perform operations which, when abstractly represented, can construct local tree diagrams or local feature tables. There are other operations by which we may interpret and represent in language semantic information, and these are cognitively just as important as those which result in representation by feature matrix or by branching tree. Among these is spatial representation.

Spatial representation is limited to three dimensions because such representation is a direct outgrowth of perception and is limited by the perceptual schemata. Such spatial representation is most obvious in the case of visual imagery, but it is certainly not dependent upon imagery. In fact, it may appear as a component of the grammatical structure of the language, or in the representation of some abstract dimensional system like that exhibited in the relations between colors (the color solid).

Spatial representation of semantic structures can be in one, two, or three dimensions. Any representation in three dimensions provides the equivalent of a model. For example, Figure 5 is a representation of part of the kinship system in English in the form of a cube having four cells. While such a cube summarizes important kin relations very well, it cannot represent the entire kin system. The kin system in a complete abstract representation requires more than three dimensions. The author (Deese, 1969) has pointed out that the full biological and social relations implied in the concept of kinship cannot properly be represented in human thinking at all. The complete kinship system is literally unthinkable. Try to imagine all the relations implied by the fact that you stand at the apex of a descent tree (you have two parents, four grandparents, eight great-grandparents, etc.), at the base of another descent tree (your children will marry, have

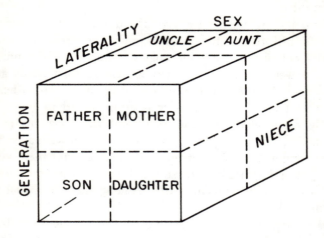

A Componential Diagram Describing a Portion of the American-English
Kin System.

children who will marry other people, etc.), and in the midst of a
laterality network composed of your brothers, sisters and cousins. In
fact, we must break kinship down into its parts and think of its parts
in different ways. To do so we adopt different semantic structures. It
should be no surprise that different cultures emphasize different
aspects of kinship and characteristically encode these in different
semantic structures. It is doubtful that many people actually think
of any part of the system of kinship as a model, but Figure 5 shows
that it is perfectly possible to do so. Furthermore, once such a representation is made, it has a curious tendency to persist. It is very likely
that the characteristic (and culturally very strange) way modern
Western societies represent the relations among colors is the result
of deliberate instruction in grade schools with the use of color wheels,
and in more advanced instruction with the color solid.

A color solid is a model, but a color wheel is a map. That is
because it is a spatial representation of certain relationships put into
two dimensions. Two-dimensional representations are extremely

common, simply because they can be so conveniently projected on a surface. Diagrams, graphs, the branching trees and feature matrices described in this chapter are all examples of attempts to represent abstract mathematical, logical, and semantic relations by spatial arrangement. It is ironic that the way we represent to ourselves the abstract structure of trees and feature matrices is by means of a map. Notice that in such representations spatial relations are usually preserved. We never put trees sideways in a book. They always read from "top" to "bottom," and we so represent them in our mind's eye. In fact, some minor conceptual confusion in linguistic theory is created by the usual tendency to perceive trees from top to bottom, and the linguist's use of an inconsistent spatial metaphor to describe an aspect of linguistic structure. The "deep" part of sentence structures are the parts near the top in the tree diagram. Sometimes students are bemused because they think the "deep" part should be the part at the bottom of the tree diagram.

Single dimensions also occur in our intellectual processes. They often have a kind of three-dimensional quality to them, but unlike the cases of models and maps, only one dimension has a direct semantic interpretation. For example we think of the best things as the "highest" and the most evil things as the "lowest." We have, in fact, an ordered scale, exemplified by the adjectival, comparative and superlative forms in the language (good, better, best), and we often metaphorically map that scale onto a dimension of physical space.

There are generally five abstract properties associated with orders and scales. They are (1) *intensity*, as in "an intense feeling," (2) *numerosity*, as in the many-few distinction, (3) *probability*, as in "he will likely come," (4) *time*, and (5) *position, length* and *size*. The last three are lumped together because linguistic representations of them often do not distinguish things that should, in exact physical representations, have more than one dimension. Consider the adjective *huge* modifying the words *success, picture*, or *box*. In the first case the representation is one dimensional, in the second two dimensional, and in the third, three dimensional. Nevertheless, we ordinarily think of those size words (*little, huge, small*, etc.) as describing something that has but a single attribute of size, irrespective of whether it is something that only metaphorically could be characterized by size ("a large mind"), or whether it is an object that varies in two dimensions ("a huge circle") or three dimensions ("a big rock"). Thus, size does not seem to be coextensive with any particular physical dimension or number of dimensions (see Deese, 1965).

What about abstract logical and mathematical relations? Do they correspond to psychologically fundamental semantic categories? Certainly some of them must, as the work of Piaget (see Flavell, 1963) on thinking in children implies. However, many operations built upon well-ordered mathematical and logical systems seem to have no special status in human thinking. We all know that the operations of ordinary arithmetic are extraordinarily difficult to perform when they exceed the limitations of ordinary perceptual experience. Children spend long tedious hours in rote practice of arithmetic operations, and yet, after all this practice, it is the rare adult who is comfortable with the request, say, to multiply in his head a pair of three digit numbers together. These same adults can easily and without hesitation produce complicated strings of sentences, interrelated with each other in a subtle and intricate way. The concepts of number, magnitude and the relationships between numbers have some very strong cognitive representation, but the operations for performing arithmetic do not.

Likewise, the abstract relations of logic have an ambiguous status in human thought. People find it much more difficult to solve syllogisms composed in abstract terms ("all Xs are Ys") than syllogisms which contain propositions about well-known things and events. However, that seems to be mainly because the syllogisms containing familiar propositions ("all men are mortal") are not solved rigorously but by the intrusion of intuition and knowledge about the world. Thus, such solutions are prone to systematic error induced by the content of the propositions in the syllogisms. People also resort to Venn diagrams to explain the relations among the terms of syllogisms. Venn diagrams are kinds of maps, and their use betrays the reliance that people place upon some spatial representation in order to apprehend the abstract relations of syllogistic logic.

The various abstract systems evidenced in mathematics and logic have as yet an undetermined counterpart in human thinking, and we must suppose that they also have as yet an undetermined role in psychological semantics. We know that the potential exists in human thought for constructing and working with various abstract systems, but we do not know the extent to which exact solution of abstract problems is first arrived at by intuition and then confirmed by various computational and algorithmic devices. In short, we neither can describe human intuition with precision nor do we know the extent to which it operates in logical thinking. The real meaning of physical theory, theoretical physicists and philosophers of science are fond of telling us, lies not in the models, diagrams, and expository prose by which most of us find out about physical theory, but in rigorously derived mathematical exposition. So whatever the limitations of human thinking, some concepts can always be referred to larger paracognitive systems built upon the mathematics and logic man has devised mostly with the aid of pencil and paper, but lately with some assistance from computers.[1]

Other choices for semantic categories come from certain operations that are both logical and linguistic. The question is whether such relations as those implied by the concepts of conjunction, disjunction, negation, etc., have semantic properties not directly given by their logical relations. Again, the representation of such concepts by diagrams, etc., suggests that this is so. For example, the concept *because*, which in traditional grammar is designated a conjunction, often has the force of logical implication. It probably is often interpreted, however, as denoting *causality*, and Michotte (1946; 1963) has demonstrated that this concept has strong perceptual reference in human experience. Also, in an analysis based entirely upon associations and therefore not fully semantic in the present sense, the author (Deese, 1965) showed that the conjunctions *and, or, but whether* seem to contrast in some fundamental way with the conjunctions

---

[1] See Johnson (1964) for an account of how high school students vary in their understanding and interpretation of abstract relations in physics.

as, if, because. It would appear that the coordinating and contrasting conjunctions contrast in some way with the conditional conjunctions, and this contrast may reflect some primitive semantic category.

The contrast in linguistic usage between negation and opposition deserves special attention in this connection, because negation has a proper and useful logical function while opposition does not. So far as logic is concerned, opposition is a special case. It is, however, more nearly the general case in language, and it provides what is perhaps the fundamental operation in the semantic category of attribute relations. Negation is, in general, an operation of specifying the complement. Thus, if I say "X is not a person," I imply the statement "X belongs to the (infinite) set of things that excludes persons." However, there is a distinctly different linguistic operation that, unfortunately, uses the same words and forms as the negative. These are the modifiers *not, un-, im-, non-,* etc. Despite the use of these modifiers to denote both the negative and the opposite, the opposite is not the complement. The nature of opposition has been discussed in the semantic literature (see, for example, Ogden 1932, 1967; Roubiczek, 1952; Lyons, 1963; Deese, 1965). And there are many reasons to distinguish it from negation. A few simple examples, however, will make a convincing case.

Two male students pass a coed. One says to another, "Not bad." The meaning is clear. Or, a harassed Dean asks the Chief of the Campus Police about the mood of the crowd and hears the answer, "Not friendly." The Dean is not being told that the crowd is everything in the world but friendly (for example, that it is large); he is being told specifically that the crowd is in an ugly mood. If I say "X is not a man," you have no real idea what X is. Or, if I say "my car is not green," you have no way of knowing what color it is. But if I say "John is not absent," you know that he is present. Or if I say, in giving you directions, "your turn is not far," you can reasonably infer the opposite of far, near. Howe (1966) shows, in the way in which people respond to the negative-oppositional modifiers, that, where a possible gradation exists, the implied opposite is not as strong as the other binary term. Thus, "not bad" is generally taken to be a little less strong, perhaps a little more restrained than an outright "good." However, the major point is that the opposite is readily inferred.

The operation of binary contrast appears to be a linguistic fundamental to which the human mind is uniquely adapted. Binary pairs of adjectives appear in all languages, and there are in English as well as related languages formal devices for inventing new adjectival contrasts. When we list the attributes which apply to a given concept, we nearly always imply that these attributes are to be thought of as being contrasted with an opposite state.

Note, however, that not all English adjectives exist in oppositional pairs. Furthermore, it is possible to think of those that do as sometimes being modified by a negational marker rather than an oppositional one. Thus, "not bad," carries a faint sense of ambiguity about it, an ambiguity that is perhaps partly responsible for its softening effect as an oppositional device. We noted above that "not green" usually implies the complement, not the opposite. Color names in English (and related languages) seem not to be paired in any simple and straightforward way. Also, adjectives which describe emotional states likewise seem not to imply the opposite. If I say "Harry is not angry," I really do not seem to be implying that Harry is in any particular state, whereas if I say "Harry is not short," it is easy to infer that Harry is on the tallish side. These exceptions of adjectives that are not paired are relatively few in English. Most adjectives have clear opposites. The notion of opposition is a linguistic fundamental, and despite its dubious logical character, permeates all languages of the world.

There remain some intriguing choices for universal semantic categories that are neither perceptual, linguistic, nor logical. Instead, they belong to the realm of human social relations. The concept of ownership, for example, is a universal one in human society, and it leads to semantic representations for which there exists no really good physical or logical equivalent. To say that my car belongs to me is logically very different from saying that X belongs to the set Y. The latter may be represented by a diagram, the former cannot, save through some purely arbitrary convention. Ownership also seems to be generalized from human experience to the world-at-large. Thus, we say that the earth "belongs" to the sun's solar system.

Ownership is merely an example of a construct defining social relations that has no counterpart outside of human society so far as we know. It is possible that those aspects of social relations that appear to be universal are represented by innate aspects of human thought and therefore choices for fundamental semantic categories. How these relations are expressed in language deserves the serious attention of students of semantics.

EMPIRICAL STUDIES OF MEANING

The traditional interest of the psychologist treating linguistic studies is in the empirical investigation of human abilities and functions in language. In this interest, psychologists have devised a number of special testing devices which are designed to explore the way in which people use words. In addition, psychologists, sociologists, and anthropologists have made cross-cultural and social studies of semantic variation. In this section we shall examine some of the methods and results in the empirical study of semantic structures.

Fixed-Response Devices in the Study of Meaning

One of the most widely used devices that psychologists have for finding out how people think about other people, ideas, and things in general is the rating scale. A particularly appropriate application of the rating scale is to the study of meaning. Rating scales are generally anchored at two ends, and this aspect of them nicely reflects the binary property of feature tables as well as the general linguistic concept of opposition. Rating scales, as a matter of fact, can be viewed as a combination of the semantic category of opposition and that of scaling or ordering.

Building upon some earlier work, C. E. Osgood (Osgood, 1953; Osgood, Suci, and Tannenbaum, 1957) adapted a more or less fixed form of the rating scale to the study of meaning. The device that resulted is known as the *Semantic Differential.* Figure 6 illustrates a standard form of the Semantic Differential. A person, in responding

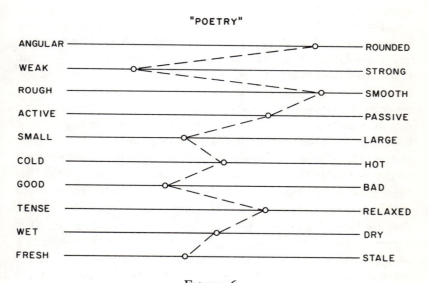

FIGURE 6.
The Ratings Supplied on a Standard Semantic Differential Form by a Single Subject Rating the Concept "Poetry."

to the Semantic Differential, indicates the degree to which a given pole on one of the rating scales applies to the concept at the top by putting a check mark along that scale. A profile for that person's idea of that concept can be made by drawing a line connecting the check marks on all the scales.

The Semantic Differential was invented in a context which made a distinction between two kinds of meaning, one denotative or objective, the other connotative or subjective. This distinction cannot be made with rigor. However, it is supposed to reflect the difference between those attributes that are inherent properties of concepts, and those attributes that show how people feel about concepts. The Semantic Differential, in its original form, was intended to show how people feel about the concepts being rated, but there is no reason in the world why it cannot be used to determine what people think are the important properties of those same concepts.

The Semantic Differential is a means for discovering the most general aspects of meaning, for we can react subjectively or emotionally to almost anything. This means that the scales of the Semantic Differential have nearly, though not quite perfect, universal applicability. Take the *good-bad* scale. It can apply to such abstract concepts as *justice* and to such thoroughly concrete concepts as *my dog*. It is not quite universal, however, for most people have a hard time deciding whether their reactions to the concept *rock* are good or bad. There is one additional defect in the fixed rating-scale form of the Semantic Differential. It is that many concepts, particularly those from a social or personal context, are complex. There might well be some aspects of a particular concept that are good and some that are bad. The form of the Semantic Differential does not allow a person who is filling it out to differentiate between the simple lack of applicability of a scale to a concept and the possibility that a concept may be mixed with respect to that scale. He must check the neutral point or something close to it, in either case.

With all of these defects considered, however, the Semantic Differential is a useful device, particularly when the correlations between the scales are taken into account. The scales applied to any sample of concepts biased in the direction of what interests people are not independent. Things that in our ordinary experience are judged to be good usually also are judged to be pleasant. That is simply the way things are. However, we must always be able to find instances of concepts for which any given pair of scales does not agree, or else the linguistic category or opposition would not work (see Deese, 1965). In general, however, people fill out the Semantic Differential in such a way so as to produce correlations between scales. The result is that the dimensions of meaning reflected in the Semantic Differential can always be reduced to fewer than the number of scales employed. The reduction of the scales to a smaller number of dimensions is accomplished through the application of some multivariate technique, such as factor analysis. In nearly all factor analyses of the data from Semantic Differential ratings, the outcome has been that three dimensions can account for most of the variation in the original ratings. These three dimensions are (1) *evaluation*, (2) *activity*, and (3) *potency*. Evaluation is best represented by the *good-bad* scale, activity is best represented by the *active-passive* scale, and potency is best represented by the *strong-weak* scale. These three dimensions, it should be noted, correspond to the three dimensions of feeling in the classical theory of feeling and emotion.

Some sample concepts which vary widely in two of the three dimensions are illustrated in Figure 7. The data for this figure were taken from ratings made by a small number of college students, and therefore the figure cannot be taken to show how people-at-large think about the concepts referred to in the figure.

The rating-scale method, as you might suppose, does not have universal applicability. For example, one way in which all concrete concepts in ordinary human experience can be characterized is by the contrast *inside-outside*. Thus, furniture is something found inside, while trees are generally found outside. But it makes no sense to scale the *inside-outside* contrast. Neither is there a reasonable scale between *married* and *unmarried*. Hence the scaling operation cannot be universally applied to all contrasts. Furthermore, as we have just seen, not all adjectives have a simple opposite (try to think, for example, of the opposite of brown). Therefore, other ways of characterizing the attribute structure of concepts are useful.

One of the best known alternatives is the Adjective Check List.[2] The Adjective Check List consists of a long list of adjectives which people check as applying or not applying to some particular concept

---

[2] There is no good single citation to the Adjective Check List. It is mainly associated with the work of V. Nowlis and colleagues at the University of Rochester.

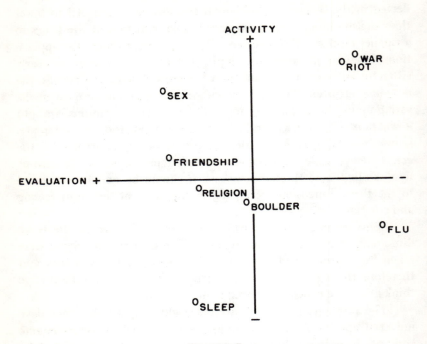

FIGURE 7.
The Results of a Factor Analysis of Selected Concepts Rated on the
Semantic Differential and Plotted in Two (Out of Three) Dimensions.

or state of feeling. The Adjective Check List has mainly been used to
study mood, but there is no theoretical reason why it cannot be put
to all the uses of the Semantic Differential. In fact, some investigators
have compared the two (see Block, 1957). However, the Adjective
Check List shares an important defect with the Semantic Differential.
Neither is a very reliable testing device when people are asked to
check denotative attributes. One would think, faced with a long list
of adjectives, that it would be relatively easy to check off those that
apply, say, to the concept of *father*. Father is surely *male*, but is he
paternal? The fact is that raters disagree, and one person may not
even agree with himself on two different occasions. Apparently there

is no fixed interpretation that can be applied to the adjective *paternal*. Some people may think that being paternal is being a beneficent tyrant, while other people may simply take it that being paternal is the state of male parenthood. Furthermore, the task of dealing with a very long list of adjectives gets to be a confusing one. It becomes curiously hard, after you have studied the applicability of two hundred adjectives to a given concept to think of what possible attributes might even apply to that concept. The net result is that there are practical limitations to the extended use of either the Semantic Differential rating scales or an Adjective Check List.

There are even more serious and universal defects with both of these methods. They are fixed-attribute methods. The person being tested must always respond to attributes put before him by the investigator. It is always possible that the investigator may miss the right attributes. Therefore, varieties of production methods may be used in place of something like the Semantic Differential.

Production Methods

The best known and perhaps the most universally employed production method is that of free association (Deese, 1962; Laffal and Feldman, 1962). Like all very general testing devices it suffers from the fact that it includes too much. A free association test consists simply of asking a person to respond to each of a number of words with the first word that comes to mind. The sum total of all the things a given person thinks of, or that a whole group of people think of, is the associative meaning of the concept behind the particular stimulus word in question. Deese (1962) and Laffal (1964) have studied the interrelationships between a number of concepts in free association. The results are sometimes interesting. It is possible to extract dimensions of meaning (see Figure 8), and the dimensions, by virtue of the particular words that group together, make sense. However, the dimensions are probably the result of all sorts of processes at work. One person will give a particular free association because one particular semantic category is at work, while another person will give a quite different response because a qualitatively

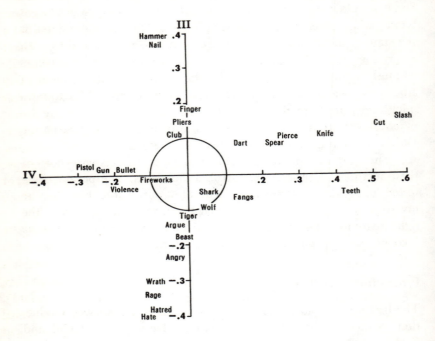

FIGURE 8.
The Dimensions of Associative Meaning for Some Words Having Aggres-
sive Connotations. There are other dimensions for these words than those
important for this collection of words. (From J. Deese, *The Structure of
Associations in Language and Thought.* Reprinted by permission of the
publisher, the Johns Hopkins Press.)

different category is at work for him. There is no way, in subjecting
the results of a free association test to any multivariate analysis, to
separate out the influence of the different categories, so that free
association remains at best a rough-and-ready technique, its chief
virtue being that it is about as context free as any psychological
probing device can be. It produces reactions from people without
forcing those reactions into any particular category.

Another productive technique is to ask people to respond with particular associative types. For example, one can ask for subordinates (Cohen, Bousfield and Whitmarsh, 1957; Battig and Montague, 1968). In so doing, one asks that people restrict themselves to but a single semantic category. The method produces a more orderly result than that achieved by free association, but one that may be artificially constrained by the possibility that people are forced to think in a way they would not think given a particular concept. The method forces a branching-tree structure. People readily think of animals, plants, and chemical elements as existing in a kind of categorical structure, but people rarely think of types of buildings for religious structures, for example, as being markers for a well-ordered set of categories. Yet, the normative information one may obtain from people will not discriminate between those reactions which are natural and those which are strained and artificial.

Finally, there are the techniques which apply multivariate analyses to judgments of similarity. These are not productive techniques though they may be used in combination with various methods of obtaining more or less unconstrained responses from people. They simply compare the patterns obtained among judgments of similarity, and they appear to result, when properly applied, in well-ordered semantic relations (see Henley, 1968). The most general judgment of similarity, though not the most convenient to analyze, comes from judgments on triads (Torgerson, 1958). In triad judgments, people are asked to indicate which among X, Y, and Z concepts are the most alike and which are most different. For example, a person, given the triad *elephant*, *cow*, and *deer*, might say that *cow* and *deer* are most alike and *elephant* and *deer* most different. There is a variety of mathematically distinct forms of multivariate analysis. Some of them yield spatial representations of similarity judgments, while others will yield branching-tree representations.

In addition to the general devices, anthropologists have invented all sorts of probing techniques for doing componential analyses of concepts held by primitive peoples, and psychologists have invented more or less exotic techniques for particular purposes. For example, the classical conditioned response may be used in an empirical study of meaning. These techniques, however, are of relatively little importance.

Cross-Cultural Semantic Studies

Many empirical investigations of semantic structures have been directed towards cross-cultural comparisons. For example, one very large investigation (see Osgood, 1964) was concerned with the comparison of the Semantic Differential among different cultures. The three dimensions that so regularly emerge in the application of the Semantic Differential to American samples also emerge in very different languages and cultures. In a sample that included among other languages, American English, Finnish, Dutch, and Japanese, Osgood was able to demonstrate that the affective-reaction system determined by the Semantic Differential has a high degree of generalizability. The particular scales that define the evaluative, active, and potent factors, of course, varied from language to language, but they nearly always emerged as the chief factors in subjective reactions to a variety of concepts. And though the scales varied, they nearly always seem to be intuitively appropriate to a speaker of American English. For example, an important evaluative scale for Japanese speakers is something that in English can be roughly translated as *elegant-vulgar*.

A few studies permit a cross-cultural comparison of semantic categories. For example, a study of Papago, an American Indian language, by Casagrande and Hale (1967), results in a list of semantic categories rather like the ones discussed earlier in this chapter. Casagrande and Hale find that Papago speakers use fourteen categories, but investigation of these categories shows that they can be reduced to a smaller number of more fundamental categories. For example, there are separate categories for function, provenience, and operations in Casagrande and Hale's analysis of Papago. But these all have the character of an attributive feature-table system.

What is interesting is that there seem to be characteristic differences between the ways in which Papago speakers and speakers of American English assign concepts to semantic categories. For example, a Papago speaker will define the nose as (1) that which is between the eyes and the mouth, and (2) as the organ for breathing. Thus, the Papago speaker first assigns a spatial description and then a class (branching tree) description. An American college student will nearly always start with the class inclusion (the organ for breathing). If his definition does code the spatial location characteristic of the nose, it will usually be by way of a class structure (the nose is a part of the face).

More radical differences between cultures are to be found in the use of various specialized semantic fields, such as that for kinship and that for color. Color terms are highly developed in the languages of Western Europe and America. Furthermore, the color-naming system is in good, though not perfect agreement, with the psychophysical relations we know to hold among colors. These psychophysical relations, we think, have nothing to do with language, but instead reflect inherent properties of the visual system. However, not all people think of color in this way; not all cultures possess color-naming systems compatible with psychophysics. The Hanunoo-speaking people of the Philippines code colors into a kind of dual system of opposites (Conklin, 1955). These people have one basic color term for long wave-length colors and another for short wave-length colors. These terms are opposites. Then there is another pair of opposites denoting the contrast between dark colors and light colors. All special color names are referred to this dual system of contrasts. The system works to name colors but it cannot be so easily mapped into the psychophysical relations of vision, and we must suppose that it does not denote colors as precisely as does our system.

There is reason to believe that coding colors by a single or by a pair of oppositional terms is more the rule than the exception among languages of the world. Of course, Western technology, including dye technology,[3] has influenced considerably the languages of the

---

[3] The author once tried to examine the hypothesis that the correspondence between our color-naming system and psychophysics arose out of the necessity of doing psychophysical experiments in the dye industry (where one must mix colors and thus do color-mixing experiments), but the history of Western color names is so complicated and so burdened with problems in historical linguistics that no simple test of the hypothesis appears to be possible.

world. For example, the Japanese language has a dual color-naming system. There is a traditional system and a "westernized" one, though by now the traditional one has been so invaded by the newer one that it is difficult to say what it is really like.

The point is, however, that a whole semantic field, such as that for color, may be referred to quite different semantic categories in different cultures. Because the color system is so highly organized, only one mode will work in a given culture, and color names, unlike other words, cannot be assigned first to one category and then another. Our color system is coded into a kind of spatial model, and that model is clearly evident in the way in which we think about colors. Some metaphorical application, however, of other kinds of sensory experience to the description of color does evoke the oppositional structure. For example, we often describe colors as warm or cool. And then, because only two of the dimensions of the color solid are in polar coordinates (hues are given in a radial system and saturation as distance from some neutral origin), there is the possibility of a contrast in the remaining linear dimension. Indeed, we do tend to think of black and white as opposites.

Other semantic fields that are highly organized and may exhibit characteristic categorical differences between cultures include kinship and folk taxonomies (animal and plant names), as well as some of the terms for human relations and feelings. None of these except kinship has been explored as thoroughly as the color case, and the kinship case brings into play special problems not really related to language. However, we do have ample evidence for genuine semantic categories and their differences, not in their absolute, but in their relative contributions to different languages of the world.

5.

THE BIOLOGICAL AND
SOCIAL CONTEXT
OF LANGUAGE

The abstract structure we call language is a product of abilities unique to the human species. It depends upon some as yet unknown characteristics of the central nervous system of man and the integration of those characteristics with the unique vocal and hearing systems of man. We know a fair amount about hearing and the mechanics of speaking, but these are matters peripheral, not central to language. The total linguistic system has been shaped by the biological inheritance of our species. But it also exists in a social context, and that social context is almost inextricably entwined with the special purposes of language. Language provides the principal means for social inheritance and the cumulation of cultural information. Therefore, this chapter considers both the biological and social context of language.

The Biological Context

Evolution and Language

Perhaps the most significant contribution of generative theory to the psychology of language is the convincing argument it presents to the effect that there must be some innate biological representation of the abstract structures of language built into the human nervous system. Lenneberg (1960; 1967) has said this predisposition has been shaped by evolution. It is, he points out, comparable to man's bipedal gait. Bipedal gait is also shaped by evolution and abstractly represented by some theoretical equivalent of an inborn neurophysiological pattern, just as the theory of generative grammar is a representation for some neurophysiological system of language. The notion of an "innate predisposition" or, more technically, some innate device corresponding to some abstract structure, does not imply that every member of the species will develop the behavior that reveals the presence of such a structure. Nor does it mean that the behavior will develop no matter what the circumstances. It is only that, given the appropriate circumstances, what we are innately fitted for will emerge readily and naturally. Hence the lack of a bipedal gait in, say, the dog, who is not equipped either by virtue of the mechanics of his body or the neurophysiological structures of his central nervous system for the production of such a pattern of locomotion. Notice, however, that a bipedal gait is nearly universal in the human species. It occurs in all cultures and at all times. Only some gross abnormality of development or some massive trauma will prevent it from being natural to a person.

Lenneberg makes four distinct points in arguing the similarity between the evolutionary status of language and that of bipedal gait. There is no variation within the species in the fundamental characteristics of language. There is, to be sure, an enormous variation between cultures in specific phonetic and syntactic patterns of language. But all human language is vocal. There are no competing media for language. Furthermore, all human languages make about the same number of phonetic distinctions. There are, in all languages, roughly forty different phonemes. There are never as many as a hundred, or never as few as ten, though there is certainly no theoretical or logical reason why there should not be. In fact, there is no purely theoretical reason why any language cannot be mapped into a system that makes a single distinction, as does, for example, the binary arithmetic notation.

Furthermore, as children we acquire phonetic systems, not just the individual sounds that are supposed to be the signals for the language we speak. Lenneberg (1960) points out the contrast between the parrot and the child in this respect. A parrot that learns Russian phrases from a Russian speaker and then learns English phrases from an English speaker will not speak English with a Russian accent. A Russian speaker, if he learns English after the age of maturation of the linguistic system (which Lenneberg places at around puberty), will invariably speak English with a noticeable accent. The child learns a whole phonemic system, not merely a sequence of phones, and that system influences any subsequent system he learns. However, the parrot merely learns a sequence of phones. All languages show concatenation (see Chapter One), and concatenation always obeys syntactic principles; it is syntactic structures that are responsible for what, at the phonetic level, can be represented as a concatenation of phonemes or bundles of phonetic features.

Lenneberg also points out that there is an organic correlate of language. That organic correlate is reflected in uniformities and universal characteristics of language. Children appear to learn languages in much the same way, no matter what the culture. There is more similarity to the grammars of children's dialects than we would have supposed from the adult grammars. There are no cultures in which children have not mastered the essentials of the mother tongue by age four. Furthermore, there is indirect evidence for the inheritability of linguistic function. Some of that evidence comes from the difficulty of formulating a theory of learning which could account for the known facts of how children use language. Other evidence comes from the remarkable degree of intra-individual stability in how children develop languages. There are very few persons who do not have the ability to produce remarkably elaborate syntactic patterns. Even individuals who are severely depressed in intellectual abilities seem to have this function. There are a few retarded individuals who are profoundly deficient in this ability, but even among these—the traditional idiot category—there is some linguistic function present in many cases. Furthermore, specific damage to the central nervous system is associated with specific deficiencies in the use or acquisition of language.

Finally, Lenneberg points out, there is no history of the development of language within the species. Languages change, but they do not become more complex or simpler. They simply change. Very primitive cultures possess languages which in subtlety and complexity are comparable with the languages of the world's most developed cultures. As far as written records go back, there is no change in the complexity of language. Other aspects of man's social world that depend upon learning and upon social transmittal do show enormous variation from culture to culture. In fact, of those aspects of civilization that we regard as culturally central, language seems to be unique in its universality and complexity and stability. The concatenation system by which man represents language is as historically static as is man's bipedal gait. Consider, by contrast, how governmental and economic institutions have undergone profound changes.

We have already remarked that language is unique to the human species. Apparently it is impossible to teach animals a code based upon the syntactic properties of human language. Young chimpanzees are able to perform feats of considerable intellectual skill, feats that are comparable in ability to those which children at the same stage of development can perform. But no one has reported success in teaching a chimpanzee to talk or to communicate in human syntactic patterns by means of some nonvocal code. It is not for want of trying. Many psychologists have spent endless hours during the past twenty-five years trying to teach chimpanzees and other animals to use language. On the other hand, a few people have suggested that some animals—the porpoise is a popular candidate—have a linguistic system perhaps different from that of human beings but comparable to it. It is hard to know what this assertion means in the technical sense, and no one has found any really hard evidence to support the existence of infrahuman languages. To be sure, ethologists and other students of animal behavior sometimes use the term language to describe instinctive patterns of communication between members of a species (the "language of the bees" is a famous example), but such communication is not linguistic in the technical sense. Perhaps many animals, porpoises included, communicate with one another, but they do not do so by a concatenated, syntactic, rule-bearing sequence of symbols. In fact, the concept of symbol is probably grossly inappropriate as applied to animal communication.

Brain Mechanisms in Language

A little over a century ago, a man came to the French physician, Broca, with the complaint that, following an accident, he had difficulty in speaking. The man died shortly afterwards, and in a subsequent autopsy, Broca discovered that there was a small focal lesion in the frontal region of the left cerebral hemisphere. An autopsy of a second case seemed to show the same correlation. Therefore Broca jumped to the conclusion that the ability to use language was located in this circumscribed region of the left cortex. A century of clinical observation and experimentation has served to alter Broca's conclusion, but there is little doubt but that the region bearing his name is one of the important parts of the brain that determine linguistic function.

First of all, the peculiar lateralization reported by Broca (language in the left hemisphere) seems to be generally correct. This makes the cerebral representation of language virtually unique among known brain functions. Speech and language seem to be localized in the left cerebral hemisphere, the motor portion of which controls the right side of the body, for most people. Because there is for most people a decided hand (and eye, ear and foot) preference, physiological psychologists have searched for some connection between hand preference, cerebral dominance and linguistic localization. That there is some relation appears to be beyond doubt, but its exact nature has escaped all efforts to describe it. The linguistic dominance of the left hemisphere is not complete. Damage in the right cerebral hemisphere (which controls the muscles of the left side of the body) does produce some residual linguistic impairment, but the extent of the impairment is much less than for comparable left cortical damage. Apparently for a few people ("true" left-handed people), the lateralization is completely reversed.

However, linguistic function is diffusely represented within the left cortex. It has no particular locus. Lesions in a wide variety of locations—almost over the whole of the left cortex—tend to be associated with one or another form of linguistic disturbance. The regularities of the association of linguistic function with various parts of the brain are hard to find. Electrical stimulation of the exposed cerebral cortex of man provides another source of information about the correlation of language and brain localization, (Penfield and Roberts, 1959). Such stimulation can be done when an individual undergoing brain surgery is free from the influence of an anesthetic because the brain itself is insensitive to pain. The surgery can be, at certain stages, accomplished under local anesthetic. In certain locations such stimulation will interfere with speech in various ways, though there is again no clear correlation between the type of interference and the location of the stimulating electrode. Also, sometimes stimulation would seem to elicit or arouse incipient speech or some particular linguistic memory.

In short, there is evidence that the cortex and parts of the cortex contain structures specialized for the production of speech. However, the nature of these structures and their relation to the various aspects of linguistic functions are not clearly understood. Although there are many available facts concerning correlation between brain damage, brain localization and linguistic function, these facts do not add up to a coherent account. Partly, the trouble is that techniques for studying brain functions are crude. As Lenneberg (1967) points out, stimulation of the conscious human brain is interesting, but the results are hard to interpret. Stimulation is a kind of abnormal interference with the ordinary activity of the brain. Localized nervous activity is initiated on the surface of the cortex from a single location, and there is no way to know how that stimulation is integrated into the ongoing activity. It is a far more difficult case than that presented, for example, by the problem of finding out how a computer works by studying its output as massive electric shocks are administered to the units in which it is housed. Nor can the studies of brain damage and linguistic deficit be easily interpreted. We do not know, in physiological detail, just what happens to the relations between brain cells when some of them do not function.

Another source of difficulty is the problem of characterizing the nature of the defects themselves. The linguistic defects do not correspond to any orderly segregation of functions that one would expect from an abstract analysis of the nature of language, and so it is very difficult to correlate what we know about the abstract structure of language with the effects of brain damage. The symptoms of linguistic deficiency as the result of brain damage are known collectively as *aphasia,* and despite their lack of precise correlation with linguistic analysis, they are interesting and important enough to warrant separate comment.

Aphasia

The most common cause of sudden loss of ability to use various aspects of language comes from cerebro-vascular accidents—strokes. In these accidents, rupture of blood vessels in the brain produces widespread damage to the brain. The first sign of such an accident may be a sudden reduction in some skill—there is no associated pain. Thus, a patient may notice that he has trouble with the muscles on one side of his body, or if aphasia is involved, that he has trouble remembering words or forming those words into sentences. The particular combination of physical, intellectual, and linguistic symptoms varies from patient to patient, and it is very difficult to find an orderly pattern.

Much of the effort to understand the various aphasic symptoms has been addressed to the simple problem of trying to classify them.

There are many alternate classifications available and only a little reason to choose among them, at least insofar as they differ in their details. Most, however, make a distinction between *receptive disorders* and *expressive disorders*. This distinction reflects the fact that aphasic symptoms much of the time appear to be characterized by either difficulty with the reception of language or difficulty with the expression of language. The disorders of reception range from an inability to hear the sounds of language to the complaint that the patient's native language is unfamiliar and "sounds like a foreign language." On the expressive side, the flow of speech may be reduced, so that the patient has to grope for words. Or, it may simply be disorganized and even speeded up in the process. The patient cannot produce sentences which make grammatical sense.

The most common and therefore the most significant expressive disturbances are various effects localized in words. Some patients cannot remember particular words, though they know what it is that they want to say. Or, in another case, a patient may persistently use the wrong word, though his choice is usually of one that is somehow related to the right word. Often the difficulty is transitory, and the patient may be able to think of the word in another context. Thus, it isn't that the memory for the particular word is lost, but simply that the patient has trouble putting together all of the semantic features that characterize the word in order to retrieve it from memory. Comparable difficulties appear on the receptive side. A person may simply be unable to recognize a word when he hears it, though he knows the concept behind the word.

Other expressive aphasic disorders are characterized by spoonerisms, agrammatical interpolations, or compulsive repetitions of a very few phrases, whether appropriate or not. Nearly all aphasic symptoms occur sometimes in normal experience. It is the extent and severity of the disturbance that causes the label aphasic to be applied. There are thus, a bewildering variety of specific symptoms, some of which are seen more or less in isolation and others of which may be combined with other intellectual and motor defects. They vary both in severity and in character. In addition, there are a whole series of related disorders of language which are not officially classed among the aphasias. These include alexia, or inability to read and agraphia, or inability to write.

For many brain lesions, particularly those that are focal rather than diffuse in nature, there will be a time change in the nature of the symptoms. In a cerebro-vascular accident, for example, the initial symptoms may be quite severe, but in the course of a few weeks or months, they may be considerably reduced in magnitude. Lenneberg (1967) points out that aphasias acquired in childhood differ radically from those acquired in adulthood in this respect. In children between the ages of four and puberty, the symptoms of aphasia which result from known brain damage are comparable to those in adult individuals. The difference is in the course of recovery. Some adults may fully recover from the signs of the symptoms, but most carry residual signs, and for a large number of people there will be little or no significant recovery. By contrast, children almost always recover completely, so that as adults they will show no detectable aphasic symptoms whatever. This fact led Lenneberg to the view that the brain's linguistic system is not fully matured until puberty. If there is damage to the system before maturity, the system is capable of developing in such a way as to compensate for the damage. However, damage after the system is completely matured cannot so easily be compensated for by further development. After puberty, there will nearly always be some residual signs of aphasia.

One of the most puzzling features of the relationship between brain organization and linguistic function is perhaps explained by the ability of the linguistic system of the brain to provide compensatory development. It is the apparent lack of congenital symptoms, comparable to those found in aphasia, in the absence of profound intellectual impairment. There is a literature on familial defects in language, but these defects are seldom reported as being anything like those that occur in aphasia. They include such things as difficulty with reading (dyslexia), stuttering, and delayed onset of speech. Some comparisons of identical and fraternal twins show that these symptoms are more likely to go together in identical than in fraternal twins (see Lenneberg, 1967). The hard facts on genetic determiners of linguistic ability are missing, however. In view of the strong emphasis that generative theory places upon the innate basis of linguistic performance, this absence of facts on genetic determiners is a serious lack in the biological study of language.

In short, we have no clear picture of the relationship between linguistic functions and their underlying biological substrate. The situation is rather like seeing the ground from an airplane through a cloud cover. Now and then we catch a glimpse of something concrete, but it is possible to put the whole together only with the application of much imagination and vague speculation. We can see that there are different kinds of disorders as the result of damage to the biological substrate of language, and that these bear a rough relation to various functional aspects of language, but we can see little more. If we knew how the damage actually affected the brain perhaps we would know more, but an equally important limitation is provided by the crudity of the devices we have for probing changes in linguistic deficiency, so the problem is psychological as well as physiological.

THE SOCIAL CONTEXT

Language is queen of all the social artifacts and systems of man. It is the transmitter of his heritage as well as the basic solvent of society. It is also determined by other cultural products of society, though our strong current emphasis upon linguistic universals (as a consequence of generative theory) should not lead us to expect that culture can make language take any conceivable form, or that languages differ in some profoundly different way from culture to culture. The intellectual concern in the relation between language and society settles on three major issues. These are: (1) language as the vehicle of social communication; (2) language as the determiner of human social structure, and (3) language as the result of social forces. Each of these deserves separate comment.

Language and Communication

Language is the chief, though by no means the only, medium of communication. Gestures, pictures, diagrams, cries, whistles, and various kinds of symbolic representations are all avenues of communication. In general, these are not like language, except in a few superficial senses. The most significant sense in which they might be said to be like language is that they are meaningful. Also, they are sometimes described as having componential or distinctive feature structure. A few linguists have supposed that gestures, for example, are analogous to phonemes in that they are composed of a few basic elements in various combinations. An important school of French literary criticism, one which incorporates some of the ideas of the anthropologist Levi-Strauss, is concerned in part with a kind of componential analysis of various nonverbal art forms and forms of communication. However, gestures (and symbols generally) are not joined together to form sequences which obey rules based upon some universal grammar and which permit the assertion of an infinite number of propositions. In a trivial sense, some gestures—those used in sign language—might be said to be language, but only because they are derived codes of real languages. Music, which is less communicative in the referential sense than gestures or symbolic art, is more like language, in that its elements (notes and harmonic combinations) are concatenated in rule-determined structures. However, no one has ever claimed that the rules of music are derived from some underlying universal grammatical system. In fact, contemporary musicologists uniformly regard the rules of music as completely arbitrary and subject to change.

Sometimes it is asserted that the various nonlinguistic modes of communication are based upon innate mechanisms. It is argued that they are produced more or less instinctively and recognized without special training. This may be partly true. Some gestures may be based upon universal, species-specific responses. If that is so, they are similar to communicative acts in other species. Some gestures are closely identified with particular emotional states, and that identification suggests a species-specific and innate origin. However, it is also the case that some gestures are arbitrary, and even gestures based upon innately determined emotional reactions are glossed over with a heavy layer of conventionality.

Psychoanalytic theorists and others have argued that certain visual forms have a universal meaning. In orthodox psychoanalytic theory, that meaning is said to derive from the resemblance of forms to sexual objects and events. However, in some other systems of psychoanalytic thought, notably that of the late Carl Jung, it is asserted that certain symbolic forms have a universal meaning not because they resemble things in the world but because they elicit certain genetically determined universal patterns of meaning. However, in the technical sense such symbols do not form a language, for they do not combine according to rule, nor are they based upon principles derived from a universal grammar.

In order for communication to take place between two or more individuals, meaning must be shared. Gestures and symbols may be shared, either because people know what they conventionally represent or because they elicit fundamental instinctive reactions. Communication in a genuine language requires that both the particular grammar of the language be shared by the communicating individuals, and that the way in which convention maps meaning onto a lexicon also be shared. The syntactic patterns for communication within a language provide a lesser problem, for they are not too numerous, and with even marked deviations from them, the forms of sentences are readily interpreted. However, the lexicon seems to have a very different status. We saw in the chapter on meaning that particular words may be interpreted by referring them to one or another semantic category. However, there is no guarantee that a speaker and his listener will refer a given word to the same category. And even if they do, they may map quite different contents onto those categories. If, for example, I say "My friend is a lady," you may legitimately infer a meaning suggesting that my friend is not just an ordinary female person but one who has some special status. Yet, in the common American dialect, the word *lady* is widely used as a genteel synonym for *woman*, and you may thus misunderstand me. Or consider "He is a politician." This can be taken as naming a person's occupation (a classificatory structure), or it can be taken as describing his consummate skill at manipulating people (an attribute structure). The problem is complicated, of course, in that the way people think about concepts behind words doesn't stay fixed, but changes from moment to moment or from occasion to occasion. Yet, despite these problems we do communicate with one another.

The fact that we can communicate partly reflects that we do not ordinarily place very demanding criteria on our interpretations. An approximately correct one will do in most cases, either because it isn't necessary to be precise or because the precision can be supplied by extra-linguistic events. For example, directions about how to do something ought to be precise, but the imprecision of such linguistic communication requires compensation in the implicit knowledge people may have, for example, of machinery or the way in which cities are laid out, or to whatever subject the directions refer. However, it should be noted that directions make very heavy demands upon language, and people often complain that carefully written directions, even when supplemented by diagrams and pictures, are difficult to follow. Tape-recorded speech is often difficult to follow for what, in part at least, is the same reason. In conversation we rely so heavily on situational, usually visual, cues, that when they are absent we may not understand the speech.

Communication, of course, depends heavily on that portion of the interpretation of words that remains stable. One remarkably useful device for determining the stable interpretations of words is the word association test (see Chapter Three). Rosenberg and Cohen (1966) have applied word-association data to a kind of communication game. In the game, one person must guess which of two words (such as *woman* and *lady*) is the correct one (correct here has a purely arbitrary significance). He does so by the information he can elicit from an informant. The informant is instructed to give single words that are somehow appropriate to the correct member of the pair. Thus, if *lady* is correct, the informant might say *gentle* or *manners*, or *lord*. If *woman* is correct, he might say *man*. *Female* would probably not be an effective item of information. The associations people give predict how easy it is to solve a given pair. Associations are weighted by their frequency of occurrence. That is to say, they reveal mostly common and commonplace ideas, the things most people think of in connection with particular words. It is this property of revealing the statistically ordinary that makes associations so useful in predicting the kinds of interpretations people will place on communications.

Associations   also   provide   some   information   about   the comparative difficulty of communication between different but related languages. Lambert and Moore (1966), in a comparison of French and English monolinguals and bilinguals, show that the fidelity of communication both across and within language communities is limited by associative discordance between and within the communities. That is to say, fidelity of communication depends on how many associations people have in common regarding vocabulary items. A comparison of associations given by French, German, and English monolinguals to common words shows a remarkable degree of similarity in the associational structures between the languages (see Russell and Meseck, 1959), and this similarity is a reflection of the high degree of similarity among these languages. As we move to a comparison of more remote languages, we should expect that the degree of associative concordance would be reduced.

The problem of translation is, of course, a fundamental one in the study of linguistic communication. That question, however, should be considered in a broader context of the interaction between language and other social and cultural artifacts. In the next section, we turn to the question of the influence of language on the nature of a culture and the characteristic modes of thinking in that culture. Part of the problem we shall consider concerns the question as to whether or not it is possible to translate ideas central to a culture into a language radically different from that language's cultural base.

Language and Culture

One of the most persistent and influential ideas in the history of linguistics is that which currently is known as the *linguistic-relativity hypothesis*. Under that name it is associated with the ingeniously and sometimes ingenuously argued ideas of the late amateur American linguist, B. L. Whorf, and his teacher, E. Sapir. *The basic premise of the linguistic relativity hypothesis is that our modes of thinking as well as the artifacts of our culture are at the mercy of the language we speak.* This notion was one of the cornerstones of early 19th-century German romantic linguistics. In fact, the idea seems to arise whenever academic linguists come into contact with languages that are exotically different. Early 19th century German scholars became aware of linguistic relativism for two reasons, both of which were byproducts of European expansion and imperialism.

One reason was the result of the contact of Europeans with the languages of India. European scholars immediately recognized that the various Hindu tongues had a strong kinship with most of the languages of Europe. That kinship was even more apparent when the classical language of India, Sanskrit, was compared with the classical languages of Europe, Greek and Latin. European scholars found it strange that there was at such a great distance a family of closely-related languages, while other languages that were much closer—Arabic, for example—were unrelated to European languages.

The second reason for awareness of linguistic relativism was that Europeans had also been coming into contact with the strange languages of America, Africa and other regions that were explored and colonized during the 18th century. Gradually, the notion came into being that there were families of languages, and it was argued that these families shared not only a common linguistic heritage but a common cultural and common biological heritage as well. The Indo-European languages were called Aryan, after the presumed primitive people who were the first speakers of the language. In this context, the dubious concept of a modern Aryan race arose. At the same time, it was recognized that there were other language families and that they were based upon radically different cultural and linguistic bases.

The Whorf-Sapir version of the linguistic-relativity notion grew out of the beginnings of modern anthropology's investigation of the languages of the American Indians, often called by anthropologists Amerind languages. Whorf's (1957) particular version of the notion was influential partly because of the appositeness and uniqueness of his examples and partly because he stated the hypothesis in a most radical way. He argued that our whole conception of the world is at the mercy of the language we speak, particularly the grammar of that language. He claimed, for example, that the Hopi Indians could never have developed anything like Aristotelian philosophy because that philosophy—in fact the whole of European philosophy—demands a separation between objects (existence) and action (motion or events). Such a distinction cannot easily be expressed in Hopi. On the other hand, the Hopi way of thinking about the object-event relation is difficult for Indo-European speakers to understand.

The heart of the distinction between the Hopi point of view and the English (as a representative Indo-European language) point of view lies in the distinction between nouns and verbs. Whorf apparently accepts nouns and verbs as representing fundamental grammatical categories, but he argues that their particular use and distinctions between them vary from language to language. Verbs in English are said to denote actions. Actions are characteristically short-lived events compared with things, that are relatively enduring events. Thus the event denoted by *strike* or *hit* is here and gone, whereas the event denoted by *a rock* is here and gone only on a scale of geological time. Yet, Whorf asks, why is *fist* a noun, since it really names an action (moving the hand into a particular formation). In Hopi the distinction between nouns and verbs is not a distinction between action and things; it is a distinction based entirely on duration. Thus *lightning, spark, wave, flame,* and *puff* of *smoke,* are verbs. Events of necessarily brief duration must be verbs. *Cloud* and *storm* are nouns in Hopi, but barely so. *House, man,* and *rock* are all definitely nouns. Thus, if Whorf is correct, a basic philosophy of nature is built into language.

Speakers of any given language can always find circumlocutions for expressing what can be expressed in another language, but such circumlocutions are sometimes awkward and difficult to understand. It is worth noting in this connection that Whorf often resorts to diagrams in order to explain the difference in linguistic structures between languages. The main argument of linguistic relativism, however, is that the habitual mode of thought is revealed in the common patterns of language. These common linguistic patterns channel our thoughts and determine the kind of culture we build.

If we accept the point of view of generative grammar, we must suppose that there is, at the bottom, a certain basic identity among languages. All the languages of the world are generated by the same kind of device, and they are built upon common principles. According to generative grammar, the structure of all sentences may be described by a set of context-free rewrite rules plus transformational operations applied to the product of the application of those rules. All sentences have a basic propositional structure which divides them into subject and predicate structures, and these in turn have constituent structures. Therefore, linguistic relativity must have severe limits according to generative theory. Generative theory has proven to be so significant in modern linguistics that we cannot ignore it. Thus, we must regard with suspicion the claims of extreme adherents of the linguistic-relativity hypothesis. These claims assert that some languages have no verbal and nominal categories at all, or that some languages do not possess subject-predicate constructions. Such assertions call upon some mysterious theory of grammar, a theory that no one has yet fully explicated, and they do not seem to lead us anywhere. Within the boundaries set by a universal grammatical generating device, however, variations in language may indeed be responsible for characteristic cultural differences in thought.

There have been a few attempts to examine the linguistic-relativity hypothesis by means of psychological studies. These, almost without exception, have been studies of semantic structures rather than grammatical ones. That is to say, they have not been concerned with the relations among the fundamental categories of different languages, but instead they have been concerned with the assignment of semantic features to words or morphemes in different languages.

The favorite semantic field for investigation has been color. We have already seen (Chapter Three) that the characteristic Indo-European color-name system has a structure that is different from those we find in technologically less-developed cultures. We tend to accept our own system as universal chiefly because it is the one with which we are familiar, and because we find that it also accords with the basic psychophysics of vision. It was hard for Western psychologists to accept the notion that other systems were possible, but once that notion was accepted, it was responsible for a number of investigations.

One of these (Brown and Lenneberg, 1954), is simply an experimental study of color naming in a representative sample of speakers of English. The study showed that the way in which people perceive and remember colors is a function of the boundaries established by the mapping of color names onto the spectrum. It is easy to identify and remember a color if it is unambiguously blue, red, or green. If, however, the color is a blue-green, a chartreuse, or magenta, it is harder to match from sample or to identify the color.

Another study compared the way English speakers map color names onto the spectrum with the kind of mapping monolingual and bilingual Navaho speakers make (Landar, Ervin, and Horowitz, 1960). The differences are considerable. Navaho speakers have one broad term that encompasses what English speakers characterize as green, blue, and even purple. The Navahos make a sharp distinction among colors at the red end of the spectrum, a distinction not unlike that made by English speakers. The reaction time in identifying colors goes along with the pattern of distinctions. Reaction times for both Navaho and English speakers are longest for those colors for which there is greatest linguistic uncertainty. For example, both Navaho and English speakers take longer to identify by name colors that fall on the boundary between green and yellow. That is because there is linguistic uncertainty for both languages in this region. Reaction times for Navaho speakers, however, are short on the boundary between green and blue, because Navaho makes no distinction between these colors. The result is that there is no linguistic uncertainty for the speaker of Navaho. English does make such a distinction, however, and so reaction times in assigning a name to a color on the boundary between green and blue are long for English speakers.

Many examples of these semantic differences can be found. They are, however, trivial alongside of the grand speculation one can easily find concerning linguistic relativism. That speculation is not limited to a comparison of languages that are, linguistically speaking, grossly different. For example, Herdan (1957) has argued that all the evil features of German national character are to be laid to what Mark Twain called the awful German language. Herdan argued, for example, that the extensive nominalization (and the universal capitalization of nouns) in German gives rise to a tendency for German speakers to reify abstractions and slogans, such as "blood and race" into an imagined concrete reality. These kinds of ideas, however fascinating they may be, seem to be beyond the techniques of empirical study, and there is no way to incorporate them into well-developed linguistic theory. They remain, then, opinion. That is the status, unfortunately, of much of the discussion of linguistic relativism. In fact, partly as the result of generative theory and partly as the result of changing attitudes in anthropology, the current emphasis is upon possible linguistic universals (see Greenberg, 1966) rather than upon linguistic relativism.

Environmental and Cultural Determinants of Language

Culture, the human environment, and language all exist in an interdependent matrix. Language influences culture and the environment (Whorf would have been interested in the use of the word *pollution* in connection with atmospheric changes induced by industrial wastes). But culture and the environment also influence language. We just mentioned the fact that the Navahos (and other southwestern Indians as well) are careless about differentiating between the short wave-length colors (green, blue, and violet) but that they are just as careful as the rest of us, perhaps even more so, in differentiating between the long wave-length colors (reds and yellows). Some people have argued that is because these Indians live in an environment in which the predominant and important colors of nature are in the long wave-length region of the spectrum.

Whorf reminded us that the Eskimos have many separate words for snow, whereas we must describe the differences in snow by combations of words (dry snow, powdered snow, wet snow, etc.). The Hanunoo speakers of the Philippines derive their color names (they divide the spectrum into a long wave-length color and a short wave-length color) from the appearance of vegetation during the two seasons of the year. The word for the long wave-length color (mostly the reds) is derived from the word for dry or desiccated, and the word for the short wave-length color (the blues and greens) is derived from the word for wet. These people live in a forest environment, and the most striking environmental change for them must be the alteration in the appearance of plants in the wet and dry seasons.

Another example of environmental determination in languages is culled from the American southwest, where nearly all Indian languages of the region (Hopi, Zuni, etc.) have but a single word for tree which is coextensive with the designation of a particular kind of tree, the cottonwood. That is because the cottonwood is really the only deciduous tree in the region. However, when the need to designate another kind of tree arises, the word for cottonwood is used. Thus, the environment influences the distinctions made by the language. It isn't that a Hopi speaker can't see the difference between a maple and a cottonwood, it is only that his language leads him to regard that difference as being unimportant.

Cultural determinants of language are even more important. Anyone who has tried to learn the paradigms of French or German verbs knows that a series of important social distinctions are built into the grammar of these languages. In French, the second person singular is said to be *tu*, while the second person plural is said to be *vous*. However, the distinction that is marked is really not number (*vous* is used in both the singular and plural) but social distinction. The rules are complicated, but in general the second person singular may be used for the singular between intimates and members of the family, or alternatively in addressing social inferiors or children. All other situations demand the use of *vous*. Essentially the same social distinction governs the use of the singular form *du* in German and the plural form *Sie*.

Many languages reserve special forms (grammatic and semantic) for addressing women, children, priests, chieftains, slaves, and other special groups. Veblen has remarked upon the preservation of archaic grammatic and semantic forms in the sacerdotal language, used mainly to address the deity. That dialect, however, has strongly influenced the learned and academic professions. Brown and Ford (1961) noted the elaborate rules governing the forms of address in American English (who calls whom by his first name). All of these examples reveal the almost inextricable intertwining of purely linguistic rules and rules governing social usage. No more obvious or revealing testimony could be found to illustrate the fact that language and other aspects of culture exist in a mutually influential network of relations.

Concluding Remarks

This chapter has been meant to illustrate the fact that language exists in both a biological and social context, and that these contexts determine the nature of language in fundamental ways. The most basic facts of human language—that, for example, it is vocal rather than gestural—are determined by the biological structures of man. Along with upright posture and manual dexterity, language is one of the evolution-determined features of man that has made culture possible. Animal culture simply does not exist, save perhaps in some very primitive form among tool-using apes. But culture is the dominant fact about the life of man, and that culture is made possible by the existence of language. What is more, the particular form of human language has influenced the nature of the culture probably more than we can tell in the absence of any other kind of culture with which to make a comparison. We do know that specific human cultures and specific languages mutually interact to channel human thought along the paths familiar to a given society. In the study of man and his society nothing is more significant than the study of language.

REFERENCES

Battig, W. F. and Montague, W. E.　*Category Norms for Verbal Items in Fifty-six Categories.* Boulder, Colorado: University of Colorado, 1968.

Bellugi, U.　(1964). Cited in McNeill, D. On Theories of Language Acquisition. In Dixon, T. R. and Horton, D. L. (Eds.). *Verbal Behavior and General Behavior Theory.* Englewood Cliffs, New Jersey: Prentice-Hall, 1968.

Berko, J.　The Child's Learning of English Morphology. *Word,* 1958, 14, 150–177.

Bernstein, B.　Aspects of Language and Learning in the Genesis of Social Process. *Journal of Child Psychology and Psychiatry,* 1961, 1, 313–324.

Bever, T. G.　Associations to Stimulus-Response Theories of Language. In Dixon, T. R. and Horton, D. L. (Eds.). *Verbal Behavior and General Behavior Theory.* Englewood Cliffs, New Jersey: Prentice-Hall, 1968.

Block, J.　Studies in the Phenomenology of Emotion. *Journal of Abnormal and Social Psychology,* 1957, 54, 358–363.

Block, J.　An Unprofitable Application of the Semantic Differential. *Journal of Consulting Psychology,* 1958, 22, 235–236.

Braine, M. D. S.　The Ontogeny of English Phrase Structure: The First Phase. *Language,* 1963, 39, 1–13.

Brown, R.　The Acquisition of Syntax. *Monographs of Society for Research in Child Development,* 1964, 29, 43–79.

Brown, R. and Bellugi, U.　Three Processes in the Child's Acquisition of Syntax. *Harvard Educational Review,* 1964, 34, 133–151.

Brown, R. and Berko, J.   Word Association and the Acquisition of Grammar. *Child Development*, 1960, 31, 1–14.

Brown, R. and Ford, M.   Address in American English. *Journal of Abnormal and Social Psychology*, 1961, 62, 375–385.

Brown, R. and Fraser, C.   The Acquisition of Syntax. In Cofer, C. N. and Musgrave, B. S. (Eds.). *Verbal Behavior and Learning*. New York: McGraw-Hill, 1963.

Brown, R. and Lenneberg, E. H.   A Study in Cognition. *Journal of Abnormal and Social Psychology*, 1954, 49, 454–462.

Chomsky, N.   Three Models for the Description of Language. *IRE Transactions on Information Theory*, 1956, IT-2, 113–124.

Chomsky, N.   *Syntactic Structures*. The Hague: Mouton and Co., 1957.

Chomsky, N.   Formal Properties of Grammar. In Luce, R. D., Bush, R. R., and Galanter, E. *Handbook of Mathematical Psychology*. Vol. II. New York: Wiley, 1963.

Chomsky, N.   On the Notion "Rule of Grammar." In Jakobson, R. (Ed.). *Structure of Language and its Mathematical Aspects, Proceedings of the 12th Symposium in Applied Mathematics*, Providence, Rhode Island. American Mathematical Society, 1961, pp. 6–24. Reprinted in Katz, J. and Fodor, J. (Eds.) *Readings in the Philosophy of Language*. Englewood Cliffs, New Jersey: Prentice-Hall, 1963.

Chomsky, N.   *Aspects of the Theory of Syntax*. Cambridge, Massachusetts: M.I.T. Press, 1965.

Chomsky, N.   Appendix A. The Formal Nature of Language. In Lenneberg, E. H. *Biological Foundations of Language*. New York: Wiley, 1967.

Chomsky, N. and Halle, M.   *The Sound Patterns of English*. New York: Harper and Row, 1968.

Chomsky, N. and Miller, G. A.   Introduction to the Formal Analysis of Natural Languages. In Luce, R. D., Bush, R. R., and Galanter, E. *Handbook of Mathematical Psychology*. Vol. II. New York: Wiley, 1963.

Clark, H. H. and Clark, E. V.   Semantic Distinctions and Memory for Complex Sentences. *Quarterly Journal of Experimental Psychology*, 1968, 20, 129–138.

Clark, H. H. and Stafford, R. A.   Memory for Semantic Features. *Journal of Experimental Psychology*, 1969, 80, 326–334.

Cohen, B. H., Bousfield, W. A. and Whitmarsh, G. A.   Cultural Norms for Verbal Items in 43 Categories. Technical Report no. 22. Storrs, Connecticut: ONR-University of Connecticut, 1957.

Conklin, H. C.   Hanunoo Color Categories. *Southwestern Journal of Anthropology*, 1955, 11, 339–344.

Cooper, F. S., Liberman, A. M., and Borst, J. M. The Interconversion of Audible and Visible Patterns as a Basis for Research in the Perception of Speech. *Proceedings of the National Academy of Science*, 1951, 37, 318–325.

Deese, J. Form Class and the Determinants of Association. *Journal of Verbal Learning and Verbal Behavior*, 1962, 1, 79–84.

Deese, J. On the Structure of Associative Meaning. *Psychological Review*, 1962, 69, 161–175.

Deese, J. The Associative Structure of Some Common English Adjectives. *Journal of Verbal Learning and Verbal Behavior*, 1964, 3, 347–357.

Deese, J. *Structure of Associations in Language and Thought*. Baltimore, Maryland: The Johns Hopkins Press, 1965.

Deese, J. Conceptual Categories in the Study of Content. In Gerbner, G. (Ed.). *Communication and Content*. New York: Wiley, 1969.

Ervin, S. Imitation and Structural Change in Children's Language. In Lenneberg, E. H. (Ed.). *New Directions in the Study of Language*. Cambridge, Massachusetts: M.I.T. Press, 1964.

Fillenbaum, S. Memory for Gist: Some Relevant Variables. *Language and Speech*, 1966, 9, 217–227.

Flavell, J. H. *The Developmental Psychology of Jean Piaget*. Princeton, New Jersey: Van Nostrand, 1963.

Fodor, J. and Bever, T. The Psychological Reality of Linguistic Segments. *Journal of Verbal Learning and Verbal Behavior*, 1965, 4, 414–420.

Garrett, M., Bever, T., and Fodor, J. The Active Use of Grammar in Speech Perception. *Perception and Psychophysics*, 1966, 1, 30–32.

Garrett, M. and Fodor, J. Psychological Theories and Linguistic Constructs. In Dixon, T. R. and Horton, D. L. (Eds.). *Verbal Behavior and General Behavior Theory*. Englewood Cliffs, New Jersey: Prentice-Hall, 1968.

Greenberg, J. H. *Language Universals*. The Hague: Mouton, 1966.

Henley, N. A Psychological Study of the Semantics of Animal Terms. *Journal of Verbal Learning and Verbal Behavior*, 1969, 8, 176–184. (Also Ph.D. Dissertation, The Johns Hopkins University) Baltimore, Maryland, 1968.

Herdan, G. *Language as Choice and Chance*. Groningen: P. Noordhoff, 1956.

Howe, E. S. The Associative Structure of Qualifiers. *Journal of Verbal Learning and Verbal Behavior*, 1966, 5, 147–155.

Jakobson, R., Fant, G. M., and Halle, M. *Preliminaries to Speech Analysis. The Distinctive Features and Their Correlates*. Cambridge, Massachusetts: M.I.T. Press, 1952, 1963.

140 PSYCHOLINGUISTICS

Jakobson, R. and Halle, M. *Fundamentals of Language*. The Hague: Mouton and Co., 1956.

Johnson, M. G. *The Distributional Aspects of Meaning Interaction in Agrammatical Verbal Contexts*. (Ph.D. Dissertation, The Johns Hopkins University) Baltimore, Maryland, 1968.

Johnson, P. E. Associative Meaning of Concepts in Physics. *Journal of Educational Psychology*, 1964, 55, 84–88.

Kjeldergaard, P. (Ed.). *Perception and Language*. Pittsburgh, Pennsylvania: University of Pittsburgh Press. In Press.

Krasner, L. Studies of the Conditioning of Verbal Behavior. *Psychological Bulletin*, 1958, 55, 148–170.

Laffal, J. *Pathological and Normal Language*. New York: Atherton Press, 1965.

Laffal, J. and Feldman, S. The Structure of Single Word and Continuous Associations. *Journal of Verbal Learning and Verbal Behavior*, 1962, 1, 54–61.

Lambert, W. E. and Moore, N. Word-Association Responses: Comparison of American and French Monolinguals with Canadian Monolinguals and Bilinguals. *Journal of Personality and Social Psychology*, 1966, 3, 313–320.

Landar, H., Ervin, S. M. and Horowitz, A. E. Navaho Color Categories. *Language*, 1960, 36, 368–381.

Lenneberg, E. H. Language, Evolution, and Purposive Behavior. In Diamond, S. (Ed.). *Essays in Honor of Paul Radin*. New York: Columbia University Press, 1960.

Lenneberg, E. H. *The Biological Foundations of Language*. New York: Wiley, 1967.

Liberman, A. M., Cooper, F. S., Shankweiler, D. P., and Studdert-Kennedy, M. Perception of the Speech Code. *Psychological Review*, 1967, 74, 431–461.

Liberman, A. M., Harris, K. S., Hoffman, H. S., and Lane, H. The Discrimination of Relative Onset Time of the Components of Certain Speech and Nonspeech Patterns. *Journal of Experimental Psychology*, 1961, 61, 379–388.

Lyons, J. *Structural Semantics*. Oxford: Philological Society, 1963.

McNeill, D. Developmental Psycholinguistics. In Miller, G. A. and Smith, F. (Eds.). *The Genesis of Language*. Cambridge, Massachusetts: M.I.T. Press, 1966.

McNeill, D. On Theories of Language Acquisition. In Dixon, T. R. and Horton, D. L. (Eds.). *Verbal Behavior and General Behavior Theory*. Englewood Cliffs, New Jersey: Prentice-Hall, 1968.

Mehler, J. and Carey, P. Role of Surface and Base Structure in the Perception of Sentences. *Journal of Verbal Learning and Verbal Behavior*, 1967, 6, 335–338.

Michotte, A. E. *La perception de la causalité.* Louvain: Institut Supérieur de Philosophie, 1946. (Republished in English translation: Miles, T. R. and Miles, E. New York: Basic Books, 1963.)

Miller, G. A. and Isard, S. Free Recall of Self-embedded English Sentences. *Information and Control,* 1964, 7, 292–303.

Miller, G. A. and McKean, K. A Chronometric Study of Some Relations Between Sentences. *Quarterly Journal of Experimental Psychology,* 1964, 16, 297–308.

Mowrer, O. H. The Psychologist Looks at Language. *American Psychologist,* 1954, 9, 660–694.

Neisser, U. *Cognitive Psychology.* New York: Appleton-Century-Crofts, 1967.

Ogden, C. K. *Opposition.* Bloomington, Indiana: Indiana University Press, 1967. (Reprint of 1932 edition.)

Osgood, C. E. The Nature and Measurement of Meaning. *Psychological Bulletin,* 1952, 49, 197–237.

Osgood, C. E. *Method and Theory in Experimental Psychology.* New York: Oxford, 1953.

Osgood, C. E. Semantic Differential Technique in the Comparative Studies of Culture. In Romney, A. K. and D'Andrade, R. G. (Eds.). *Transcultural Studies in Cognition. American Anthropologist* special publication. 1964, 66, #3 Pt. 2.

Osgood, C. E. Toward a Wedding of Insufficiencies. In Dixon, T. R. and Horton, D. L. (Eds.). *Verbal Behavior and General Behavior Theory.* Englewood Cliffs, New Jersey: Prentice-Hall, 1968.

Osgood, C. E., Suci, G. J. and Tannenbaum, P. H. *The Measurement of Meaning.* Urbana, Illinois: University of Illinois Press, 1957.

Penfield, W. and Roberts, L. *Speech and Brain Mechanisms.* Princeton, New Jersey: Princeton University Press, 1959.

Premack, D. and Schwartz, A. Preparations for Discussing Behaviorism with Chimpanzee. In Miller, G. A. and Smith F. (Eds.). *The Genesis of Behavior.* Cambridge, Massachusetts: M.I.T. Press, 1966.

Rosenberg, S. and Cohen, B. D. Referential Processes of Speakers and Listeners. *Psychological Review,* 1966, 73, 208–231.

Roubiczeck, P. *Thinking in Opposites.* Boston: Beacon Press, 1952.

Russell, W. A. and Meseck, O. R. Der Einfluss der Assoziation auf das Erinnern von Worten in der deutschen, französischen und englischen Sprache. *Zeitschrift für experimentelle und angewandte Psychologie,* 1959, 6, 191–211.

Savin, H. and Perchonock, E. Grammatical Structures and the Immediate Recall of English Sentences. *Journal of Verbal Learning and Verbal Behavior,* 1965, 4, 348–353.

Skinner, B. F. *Verbal Behavior.* New York: Appleton-Century-Crofts, 1957.

Slobin, D. Early Grammatical Development in Several Languages with Special Attention to Soviet Research. In Weksel, W. and Bever, T. G. (Eds.). *The Structure and Psychology of Language.* New York: Holt, Rinehart and Winston, 1968.

Stolz, W. S. A Study of the Ability to Decode Grammatically Novel Sentences. *Journal of Verbal Learning and Verbal Behavior,* 1967, 6, 867–873.

Torgerson, W. *Theory and Method of Scaling.* New York: Wiley, 1958.

Whorf, B. L. *Language, Thought and Reality.* New York: Wiley, 1957.

ANNOTATED
BIBLIOGRAPHY

The following is a highly selective list of books which the student interested in further work in psycholinguistics will find useful.

Bloomfield, L. *Language*. New York: Holt, Rinehart & Winston, 1933. This is the most famous single work in the American structuralist tradition of linguistics, a tradition that has been all but superseded by modern linguistic theory. The student will find, however, that many ideas important to psycholinguistics still owe much to Bloomfield. The psychologist will find Bloomfield's behavioristic bias to be familiar, and a reading of Bloomfield may help to explain why the reaction of the generative theorists to older linguistic theories is of importance to psychology.

Chomsky, N. *Aspects of the Theory of Syntax*. Cambridge, Mass.: MIT Press, 1965. The most complete general statement of Chomsky's version of generative theory. This is not an easy book to read, but it does not, as do some of Chomsky's articles, make mathematical demands upon the reader.

Chomsky, N. *Syntactic Structures*. The Hague: Mouton, 1957. Much of the theory in this book has been superseded by other notions. However, this book still is influential in psycholinguistics, since it makes use of the idea of the "kernel sentence," now rejected in linguistic theory proper, but still present in much thinking about the psychology of language.

Chomsky, N. and Halle, M. *The Sound Patterns of English*. New York: Harper and Row, 1968. The long-awaited application of generative theory to the sounds of language. An extended and difficult treatise, but one that is essential to a modern understanding of the possibilities for the perception of the sounds of language.

Chomsky, N. and Miller, G. A. Introduction to the formal analysis of natural language. In Luce, R. D., Bush, R. R., and Galanter, E. *Handbook of Mathematical Psychology.* Vol. II. New York: Wiley, 1963. An introduction to some of the mathematical background of modern linguistics. This and some of the other chapters relevant to language in this volume can be followed with some perseverance even for those without too much formal mathematical background.

Dixon, T. R. and Horton, D. L. (Eds.). *Verbal Behavior and General Behavior Theory.* Englewood Cliffs, New Jersey: Prentice-Hall, 1968. This book is the result of a symposium concerned with the confrontation between traditional behavioral theory and modern generative theory in psycholinguistics. The chapters in the psycholinguistic section as well as in some of the other sections make interesting reading for someone with only a slight background in modern psycholinguistics. The quarrels generative theorists have with traditional psychological theory are made quite explicit.

Fodor, J. A. and Katz, J. J. *The Structure of Language: Readings in the Philosophy of Language.* Englewood Cliffs, N. J.: Prentice-Hall, 1964. A book of readings in modern philosophy of language. Some of the individual papers have not appeared elsewhere. Most of the papers are by linguists of the generative school, but papers by such nongenerative philosophers as Quine also appear. This is perhaps still the best single account of the varieties of modern concern—linguistic, psychological, and philosophical—with language.

Gleason, H. A. *An Introduction to Descriptive Linguistics.* New York: Holt, Rinehart & Winston, 1961 (Rev. Ed.). A standard textbook in linguistics. It shows some awareness of modern linguistic theory but is not much influenced by it. The book does reveal, however, the range of interests of modern linguists. The student interested in linguistics as a field of study will find this book useful.

Greenberg, J. H. *Language Universals.* The Hague: Mouton, 1966. An interesting little book devoted to the characterization of those features of language that are universal across all languages for nontrivial reasons. Particularly interesting are the discussions of semantic universals.

Lenneberg, E. H. *The Biological Foundations of Language.* New York: Wiley, 1967. It is unlikely that anyone else will write in the near future so thorough an account of the biological (including anatomical and physiological) background of language. An important feature of the book is an appendix by Chomsky giving a summary of a recent version of generative theory.

Miller, G. A. and Smith, F. (Eds.). *The Genesis of Language*. Cambridge, MIT Press, 1966. A symposium book, this time on development of language. This is probably the best single source for current psycholinguistic views on development.

Index

147